Cosmic
CRYSTALS

)))) ● ((((

rituals and meditations
for connecting
with lunar energy

ASHLEY LEAVY

FAIR WINDS

Brimming with creative inspiration, how-to projects, and useful information to enrich your everyday life, Quarto Knows is a favorite destination for those pursuing their interests and passions. Visit our site and dig deeper with our books into your area of interest: Quarto Creates, Quarto Cooks, Quarto Homes, Quarto Lives, Quarto Drives, Quarto Explores, Quarto Gifts, or Quarto Kids.

First Published in 2019 by Fair Winds Press, an imprint of The Quarto Group, 100 Cummings Center, Suite 265-D, Beverly, MA 01915, USA.
T (978) 282-9590 F (978) 283-2742 QuartoKnows.com

Fair Winds Press titles are also available at discount for retail, wholesale, promotional, and bulk purchase. For details, contact the Special Sales Manager by email at specialsales@quarto.com or by mail at The Quarto Group, Attn: Special Sales Manager, 100 Cummings Center, Suite 265-D, Beverly, MA 01915, USA.

23 22 21 20 19   1 2 3 4 5

ISBN: 978-1-59233-885-6

Digital edition published in 2019
eISBN: 978-1-63159-743-5

Library of Congress Cataloging-in-Publication Data

Names: Leavy, Ashley, author.
Title: Cosmic crystals : rituals and meditations for connecting with lunar energy / Ashley Leavy.
Description: Beverly : Fair Winds Press, 2019. | Includes index.
Identifiers: LCCN 2019020191 | ISBN 9781592338856 (pbk.)
Subjects: LCSH: Crystals--Psychic aspects. | Crystals--Miscellanea. | Moon--Miscellanea.
Classification: LCC BF1442.C78 L43 2019 | DDC 133/.2548--dc23 LC record available at https://lccn.loc.gov/2019020191

Photography: Jennifer Birge | coralantler.com

Printed in China

To my husband and family for their love and encouragement. To Lucy, Lauren, and Charlotte for their constant support and for always making me laugh. To my little team at Mimosa (Luna, Beki, Chris, Latasia, Lydia, Payton, and Jolie) for all their hard work and amazing spirit. To Jennifer Ann for her amazing photography skills and for making my vision come to life. And for my students at the Love & Light School for sharing in my excitement about this project.

Contents

Introduction 6

How to Use This Book 8

CHAPTER 1
Crystals & Moon Magic 11

CHAPTER 2
Crystals for the Lunar Cycle 29

CHAPTER 3
Crystals for the Lunar Zodiac 59

CHAPTER 4
The 13 Full Moons of the Year 89

CHAPTER 5
Crystals for the 13 Modern Moons 101

CHAPTER 6
Crystals for the 13 Native Moons 129

CHAPTER 7
Crystals for the 13 Celtic Moons 157

Glossary 184

Further Reading 187

About the Author 188

About the Photographer 189

Index 190

Introduction

About four years ago, my life was interrupted dramatically when I needed to have a full hysterectomy just two weeks before my twenty-ninth birthday. This wasn't entirely devastating for me because I had long before decided not to have children, but it hit me in quite an unexpected way.

My choice not to bear children felt positive and somewhat empowering, but when that choice was completely taken away part of me grieved what may have been lost. Over the next few years, I struggled silently with grieving a part of myself that I hadn't realized was so important to me. It felt like part of my feminine energy had left when my womb was removed.

Being active in the modern spiritual movement, I couldn't help but be surrounded by amazing women who were creating change by empowering one another and celebrating their womanhood. The women's movement that was (and is still) taking place is SO inspiring, but on a personal level I was still dealing with a wound that needed healing. All around me women were celebrating their womanhood, their ability to create and birth new things into the world, and their bodies.

Although my logical mind told me I was still as feminine and womanly as ever, the wounded part of me felt "less than" or incomplete. I felt a longing for a reconnection with the part of myself that had been lost. These feelings completely took me by surprise, but I knew I needed to do something to feel empowered again.

So my journey into reconnecting to the divine feminine began. I spent my days meditating, connecting with different goddesses, and creating rituals for myself. Naturally, my love of crystals ensured they were a regular part of just about everything I was doing, but I started to develop a new passion: I became enamored with the moon. I fell in love with learning all I could about staying in rhythm with her natural cycles and flows. Perhaps the need for that connection arose from the absence of my own feminine cycle, or perhaps I was simply awakening to something larger taking place in our world. Whatever the reason, living in alignment with lunar energy became part of who I am.

I spent many, many hours journaling and sketching and doodling about the spiritual moon work I was doing. One evening while connecting with some amazing women in an online Goddess Circle,

I shared a few of the ways I had been working with the moon in my own spiritual practice. It was then that I realized just how powerful this work was—and just how much I needed to share it with others as part of my own journey toward wholeness and completion.

I realized in that moment of sharing that it was not just me who was feeling disconnected from the natural world, from the seasonal cycles, and from my own divine energy. Many other women (and men!) were feeling the same way. We have become so far removed from our roots that we have forgotten how to live in harmony with the world around us. One of the easiest ways to repair this connection is to live in alignment with the moon—to let her guide our actions and become aware of our place in this universe once again.

It's with great excitement and love that I write this now, hoping you'll enjoy every ounce of goodness in these pages, hoping that you'll feel more whole, more connected, and more aligned after reading them, and hoping that you'll discover something new that excites and inspires you to share part of yourself with those who need to hear your story.

Wishing you many moons of health, happiness, and peace,
Ashley

How to Use This Book

This book is divided into seven chapters to help you better understand the energy of the moon, and how to work with that energy and harness it using crystal rituals.

Chapter 1, "Crystals & Moon Magic," provides a foundation for understanding the importance of lunar energy in your day-to-day life. It offers an explanation for how and why crystals make such perfect companions for your journey toward lunar connection. You'll learn the basics of why crystals are so powerful and how to start working with them. You'll also discover why our ancestors placed such great emphasis on our nearest celestial neighbor, the moon. This chapter sets the stage for the rituals, ceremonies, and meditations provided later in the book; it shares important techniques for crystal cleansing and space clearing, as well as for grounding and centering yourself. These techniques should always be carried out before performing the rituals described in later chapters.

In chapter 2, "Crystals for the Lunar Cycle," you'll dive deep into the eight moon phases. You'll learn about the distinct phases in the lunar cycle and how each one relates to you here on Earth. You'll also discover the unique energies and characteristics associated with each phase and how you can work with crystal energy to stay in harmony with lunar energy during each stage in the cycle. The lunar cycle is a metaphor for the natural ebb and flow that occurs in your own life. By aligning yourself with the phases of the moon and working with the energies that accompany each, you'll find that you're more aligned with the world around you.

The third chapter, "Crystals for the Lunar Zodiac," takes you on a journey through the cosmos, following the moon's orbit through each astrological house. While the moon is in each sign, it takes on, and magnifies, that sign's energetic qualities. Understanding this astrological influence on the moon can help you interpret how this energy can affect you day-to-day, based upon your own moon sign. You'll discover crystal rituals and meditations for strengthening the positive aspects of this influence on your moon sign, and you'll become aware of the less compatible aspects of each sign's energy with your own.

Chapter 4, "The 13 Full Moons of the Year," gives you an introduction to the powerful monthly moons that hold great promise and potential, especially when paired with crystal energy. Since long ago, people from cultures and traditions around the Earth have been naming the full moons of the year. These names helped tell the story of what important events would take place during each month. They connected people to the seasons and to natural cycles. This chapter also explains Blue Moons and how to understand the lunar year, which has thirteen moons, even though most people follow a twelve-month calendar.

Chapters 5 through 7 provide simple crystal rituals for connecting with lunar energy each month. Chapter 5 shares the 13 modern moons. Chapter 6 offers insight into the 13 Native moons, and chapter 7 describes the 13 Celtic moons. The traditional name and history of each monthly moon is given in these chapters, as well as the best crystals for each and how to work with them in ritual. For example, chapter 6 describes the monthly Native moons from January to December as well as the thirteenth moon (the Blue Moon), whereas chapter 7 gives the Celtic names for each. These chapters provide the deeper understanding you need to work with crystal energy for each of these full moons as they occur during the year.

CHAPTER 1

Crystals & Moon Magic

When you understand the effect that lunar energy has on your mind, body, and spirit, it's easy to see why you need a relationship with the moon. Living in sync with the rhythm of the lunar cycle is a powerful way to stay balanced and aligned with universal energy. Healing crystals, which are natural amplifiers of energy, can enhance your connection to the moon.

What Are Healing Crystals?	12
Creating Sacred Space with Crystals	14
Space Clearing & Cleansing Your Crystals	16
Crystals for Energy Clearing	19
Grounding & Centering	20
Working with Crystals	22
Understanding Lunar Energy	24
The Ebb and Flow of Lunar Energy	25
A Brief History of Lunar Ritual and Ceremony	26
Combining Crystals and Moon Magic	27

What Are Healing Crystals?

Healing crystals can be used to restore balance among your body, mind, and spirit. They're considered to be effective energy-healing tools for chakra balancing, removing energy blockages, manifesting, enhancing meditation, aligning with astrological energies, facilitating a connection with deities or spirit guides, and more.

Humankind's use of crystals dates back thousands of years, and it spans cultures and civilizations across the globe, including the ancient Egyptians, the Romans, and Siberian shamans. Although crystals have a long history of use, you may be wondering how they work and why you should bother using them today.

Most crystals form inside the Earth after intense heat and pressure facilitate the process of nucleation. Crystals are minerals that follow a geometric, structural blueprint when they form. Their atoms and molecules follow a repeating pattern until they form to completion. This special, geometric arrangement of molecules gives the crystals a perfect (or nearly perfect) structure, and it makes them highly stable in terms of their energetic vibration.

This stable energetic vibration is thought to be the way that crystals can make positive changes in the human energy field. When the perfect, stable energy frequency of the crystal is brought into your energy field, your molecules start to move into alignment with the more balanced energy. The process of your body's energy changing to match the higher vibe crystal is called entrainment. It's the universe's natural way of bringing discordant energies into balance.

Another theory about how crystals work for healing is based on their relationship with light energy. Because crystals receive, store, and send light energy, they are thought to amplify energy of all kinds. When this amazing way of harnessing energy is combined with the power of thought from the human mind, the resulting energy is phenomenal.

Because of their ability to receive energy from your mind, crystals are a great addition to your spiritual practice as a point of focus, to facilitate personal transformation and spiritual growth.

Each crystal has its own individual energy blueprint, which is why different types of stones can influence you in different ways. Because of these unique energy signatures, your experience with a particular stone will be completely unique to you. Although other people may have similarities in their shared experiences, no two encounters with a crystal will ever be exactly the same. This makes crystal healing highly subjective, as well as hotly debated. If you approach your crystal and ritual work with an open mind, you'll be pleasantly surprised with the results (and possibly full of even more questions).

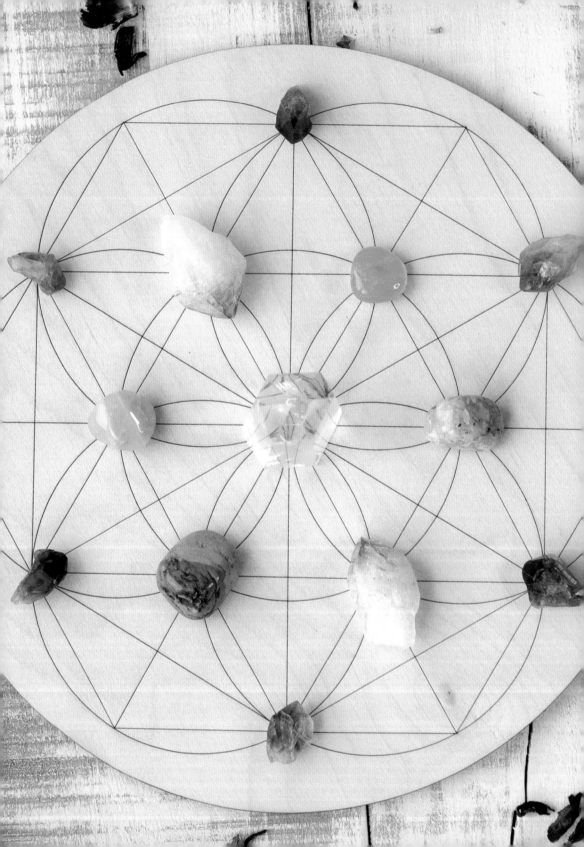

Creating Sacred Space with Crystals

Your sacred space is a special place for you to recharge and rejuvenate. It's a place where you feel comfortable and at ease—a place where you can connect to the universe. It's like having a personal sanctuary for your spirit.

For most people, a sacred space is a physical location, such as a small room or a corner of your living space. Your sacred space may contain ritual objects or personal items that help you feel more connected to your spiritual side. These items could include, for example, candles, incense, crystals, seashells, feathers, images of inspirational people, deity statues, uplifting quotes, spiritual or religious symbols and artwork, and meaningful personal items such as family heirlooms.

Whatever you choose to include in your sacred space should be a source of strength and inspiration. It should help make it feel like a special place where you can connect with the universe for healing, relaxation, and wellness. Just keep it personal and include items that are meaningful to you. Don't feel pressured to add something to your space just because others do, and don't exclude a meaningful item just because no one else has one in their sacred space. It's perfectly fine to strike a balance between traditional and personal, and it's equally okay to go full throttle with your self-expression as long as you're happy with the result.

Healing crystals are important and powerful tools for creating sacred space. One of the easiest ways to pull together all the components of your sacred space is to create a crystal altar. This is a special place in your sacred space, usually atop a small table, that is reserved for your spiritual tools. Place your incense or candles, photos, statues, and crystals on your altar to create a point of personal power. If you don't have much space to devote to your altar, use a tiny shelf, or even a windowsill, to create your altar. Just work with what you have available. The most important consideration is to place your altar where you'll see it frequently so that you can be reminded of its meaning each time you are near it.

Some of the best crystals to incorporate in your sacred space include:

ANGELITE Angelite creates a calming space where you can feel at peace. It calls in your angels and spirit guides so that you can relax, knowing you're being cared for by these loving beings.

AQUAMARINE Aquamarine helps you release any stress or worry you may have brought into your sacred space when you entered. It helps you get settled in your environment and go with the flow. It's an excellent relaxation crystal.

ROSE QUARTZ Rose Quartz is a supportive and nurturing stone that helps you feel relaxed and at ease in your sacred space.

Space Clearing &
Cleansing Your Crystals

Over time, places and objects pick up on the energetic vibrations that inhabit or surround them. Emotionally charged energetic debris or psychic energy gets stuck in the energy field of any person, place, or thing that's nearby. This debris clutters up the base energetic frequency of the object and makes it more difficult for your energy field to detect its healing energy. The most effective solution is to cleanse the object or the space with ritual clearing.

Cleansing an object or a place removes all the unwanted energy, the energy that's not for your highest good. This allows the true energy frequency to shine forth so your body can use it for healing.

Crystals, especially, need frequent cleansing because of their ability to receive and store the energy they encounter. Many people refer to this as "negative" energy, but in a realistic sense, there is no positive or negative connotation to the energy itself. There is simply energy that's for your highest good and lifts you up, and energy that's not. Regardless of how you describe it, the unwanted energy that's been accumulating in your crystals since you last used them isn't something you want mucking up your energy field. Cleansing your crystals before and after each use is highly recommended.

One of the most powerful methods of energy cleansing is smudging, the burning of sacred herbs such as sage, sweetgrass, cedar, or palo santo to remove any stagnant or unwanted energy. Items are passed through the purifying smoke of the burning herbs, or the smoke is wafted throughout a space that's being cleansed.

Smudging Ritual Place a smudging herb such as white sage or palo santo in a fireproof container, and light it on fire with a match. Blow out the flame, and waft the smoldering embers to create smoke. Pass your crystals through the smoke to cleanse them, and then carefully walk around your space with the container to clear the space.

Clearing Your Space with Crystals To use crystal energy to keep your sacred space a negativity-free zone, try placing stones on your altar, setting them around the room, storing them with your tarot cards or healing tools, and/or setting up a crystal grid—a special arrangement of crystals in a sacred geometric shape—around your entire room (or just on a table).

Crystals for Energy Clearing

Many crystals can be used to help keep your sacred space free from unwanted energy, but these are the top five best cleansing stones.

BLACK TOURMALINE This crystal is a powerful protector. It transmutes negative energy into positive vibes and keeps your space free from unwanted energy. Add this stone to your space when you're feeling crabby, reactive, or combative. Chances are, you're being affected by excess psychic debris and emotionally charged energy that's lingering in your space. By bringing a Black Tourmaline crystal into your environment, you should see a speedy improvement in the way you feel.

CARNELIAN This cleanser is known for its ability to keep unwanted energy at bay. Carnelian is often used by healers and psychics to keep their energy-healing tools cleansed. Try popping a piece in with your tarot or oracle cards, or display a piece on your altar to keep the vibrations high.

ROSE QUARTZ This gentle stone keeps the energy in your space sweet and light. Rose Quartz works especially well for harmonizing the energy of group or shared spaces to extend the time needed between deeper energy clearing.

SCOLECITE Scolecite is a relatively uncommon stone, but it is a powerful cleanser. This crystal radiates with white light and repels any dark energies that may be trying to settle into your space. Bring this crystal into your space if you need to set protective boundaries for difficult people or to keep away the negatively charged energy brought on by passive-aggressive people in your space.

SELENITE Keeping a piece of Selenite in your sacred space is highly recommended. This crystal is well known for its space-clearing abilities. It will work nonstop to keep your space free of negative vibes. It will also call upon your angels and spirit guides to assist with protection if needed. Placing a Selenite wand on each wall of your sacred space works as a negativity barrier.

Grounding & Centering

Worry, anger, anxiety, fear, and similar feelings aren't aligned with your authentic self, so when you shift your energy away from them by grounding and centering yourself, you move into a natural place of joy. This practice removes negative thought forms and emotional debris from your energy body, keeping you happier and healthier. It is an important practice for any type of spiritual work.

GROUNDING EXERCISE

The best way to align yourself with the Earth's energy is to ground yourself. Practicing regular grounding exercises will keep you free from negative thoughts and emotions.

Place the soles of your feet flat on the floor and hold a Black Tourmaline crystal or a piece of Petrified Wood. You may be sitting or standing during this exercise. Take a deep breath in, letting your belly go soft and fill with air. Hold this breath for a few seconds, and then exhale. Continue this deep breathing. On your next exhalation, visualize your legs slowing changing into tree roots. See the roots grow longer and longer, extending down toward the core of the Earth. Once they reach the center, take a deep breath in. See yourself pulling energy into your root legs, drawing it upward into your body.

Continue deep, even breathing. On your next inhalation, visualize green light filling the area of your Heart Chakra. As you exhale, consciously direct the energy down your body, through your root legs, and into the earth. Visualize your Crown Chakra opening up and drawing in universal energy. Feel the energy move into your physical body, down through your root legs, and into the Earth. Visualize your root legs loosening their grip on the Earth around them. Feel them shrinking smaller and smaller, moving back through the layers of Earth until they resume being your own legs. Take a few more deep, even breaths. When you feel ready, wiggle your fingers and your toes, come back to everyday awareness, and open your eyes.

Centering Exercise To center yourself and keep yourself focused on the present moment, try tapping your thymus. Tapping is a gentle thump on the body using the tips of the fingers. Try gently tapping your thymus (your breastbone in the area of your Higher Heart Chakra) for approximately thirty seconds to calm your mind, quiet any mental chatter, and get focused on the present moment.

Working with Crystals

There are many rewarding ways to incorporate crystal work into your life and spiritual practice. Creating crystal altars, setting up crystal grids, making crystal medicine bags, meditating with your stones, performing ritual work or ceremony, and wearing gemstone healing jewelry are just a few ways to work with your stones. But before you dive in, here are a few things you need to know.

CLEANSING You should always cleanse a new crystal when you get it. Your stones pick up on the energies they're exposed to. If those energies don't resonate with you, the experience of working with your new stone can be less than pleasant. Give a new crystal an initial cleanse, and be sure to cleanse it before and after each use when you're first starting out and may not yet be able to sense the energy of the stone. After you've grown accustomed to sensing or intuiting when a crystal needs to be cleansed, you can leave the frequency up to your intuition and inner guidance. There are many methods of cleansing, from sound cleansing with singing bowls or tingshas, to sea salt, to water, to mantra chanting—and everything in between! If you need instructions about how to cleanse your stones, see page 16.

GROUNDING & CENTERING Ground and center yourself before performing any of the rituals or meditations in this book (or any ritual work or meditation, for that matter). Grounding keeps you protected and rooted into the Earth, while centering keeps you in the present moment. Both are useful skills to have mastered before diving into crystal ritual and meditation; they will ensure that you have deeper, more meaningful experiences with each. For grounding and centering exercises, see page 20.

SETTING INTENTIONS Setting an intention may seem like something that only needs to be done when creating a crystal grid or when programming your stones. However, doing it before you work with your stones in any capacity can help you get so much more than you normally would from your crystal work. Set an intention before you meditate, before you create a medicine pouch, before you put on a piece of jewelry, or before you begin a ritual. The act of intention setting brings clarity to the task at hand, and it allows you to focus on what's important to you and why you're truly doing this work. Creating a ritual around your intention setting may also prove helpful. It doesn't have to be elaborate. Perhaps, for example, you light a stick of your favorite incense, put on some dreamy music, and write your intention on a piece of paper. Give your intention-setting routine tons of love and you'll see how good it feels to bring it into your regular practice.

Understanding Lunar Energy

The moon may not speak, but she can teach you many things if you're patient and attentive. The ebb and flow of the lunar cycle is a guide for the periods of activity and rest that you experience in your own life, on both a daily and a seasonal scale.

Most modern people don't give the moon a second thought when planning activities and projects or considering how to spend time, even though our ancestors relied upon it to determine the timing of religious and cultural festivals, agricultural activities, and magical workings. This separation from the rhythms of nature and lunar energy has left many feeling anxious, overwhelmed, and disconnected from spirit and the world around them.

When you fully understand the effect that lunar energy has on your mind, body, and spirit, as well as how much living in harmony with natural cycles affects your well-being, it's easy to see the importance of returning to a more primal, ancient relationship with the moon.

Facilitating a connection to the moon and her energies will help you cultivate a deeper understanding of yourself on a soul level. Tuning into the moon is about self-exploration as much as it is about discovering the dynamic energy of Lady Luna.

Reclaiming your wisdom of the moon can fuel a personal journey of self-discovery, inner work, and soul-level healing. Most of this deep transformation comes from getting involved and active with lunar energy. Ceremony, ritual, meditation, and connecting with your crystals are all important parts of developing this skill and pushing ever further into the cosmic energy that inspires so much of who you are and how you engage with the world around you.

This journey starts with a commitment to being more conscious of lunar energy, paying attention to this prominent celestial body, and learning what she has to share with you.

The Ebb and Flow of Lunar Energy

Living in harmony with the moon cycle and the innate qualities of the moon's energy will inspire you to live a more soulful life. Let the moon inspire you to:

- develop your intuition
- discover your inner self
- take time for relaxation
- retreat inward
- be at ease with your body
- create with wild abandon
- feel true excitement
- dream fearlessly
- leave behind what doesn't serve you
- manifest prosperity
- live passionately
- enjoy the present moment
- get out of your head
- achieve greater success
- take risks
- awaken to new possibilities
- nurture your spirit
- be mindful
- value spontaneity
- release your baggage
- attract more abundance
- get inspired
- practice gratitude
- maintain boundaries
- expand your knowledge
- create deeper personal relationships
- let go of things that are holding you back
- focus on healing
- inspire others

A Brief History of Lunar Ritual and Ceremony

Moon magic has been a common practice since further back in time than anyone can pinpoint. Humankind has always been fascinated with the energy of our nearest cosmic neighbor.

People from almost all world cultures have placed great significance on the movements and phases of the moon. Ancient Egyptian philosophers, for example, used the moon phases to track the passage of time and create some of the first lunar calendars. They used this information to determine when to plant and harvest crops. The moon plays a prominent role in the mythology and religions of many ancient and modern spiritual traditions—from ancient Egypt and Babylonia to modern Hinduism and Paganism. Some of this lunar tradition and cosmology has been lost to us, but some has made it through. A brief look into ancient art and writing reveals myriad beliefs about the moon, associated deities, and how humanity was influenced by the moon's energy. The ancient Egyptians, Taoists, Celts, Native peoples from the Americas, Hebrews, Chinese, Babylonians, Indians, and many others make reference to the importance of the moon in society and in spiritual practice.

Although some modern moon rituals may be loosely based on tradition, much of today's moon-based ceremony is created through intuitive inner guidance and personal preference. You can practice your own deeply personal moon ritual to connect you with lunar energy.

You'll find many modern moon rituals throughout this book to help you align with the phases of the moon, the Lunar Zodiac, and the thirteen full moons of the year. Feel free to follow these rituals as described, or customize them and make them your own. Add things that you feel called to include, or skip over parts that don't resonate with you. This is about enhancing your connection to the moon and her natural rhythms, so don't be afraid to make changes and do what works best for you.

Combining Crystals and Moon Magic

When you're working with lunar energy, healing crystals can strengthen your connection to the moon and allow you to experience moon vibes in a deeper way.

Because crystals are natural amplifiers of energy, they boost your emotional connection to your ritual work, thus profoundly enhancing your experience. Additionally, healing stones can stimulate your intuition and awaken your innate psychic abilities. This intuitive boost allows you to perceive more about the subtle cosmic energies than you normally would, giving you further insight into your relationship with the moon.

Healing crystals can be used to give you a tangible connection to the energy of the moon phases, the Lunar Zodiac, and the full moons of the year. Although the moon's energy feels quite noticeable for those who have started to develop a relationship with her, having a physical connection to that energetic wavelength helps reinforce your feelings, intuition, and experiences.

The moon is dynamic and constantly changing, just like the Earth is. Crystals seem to be natural companions to the moon; using them to work with spiritual themes and key energies feels quite natural. Having this special way to relate to and work with lunar energy makes the experience more rewarding and enriching.

CHAPTER 2

Crystals for the Lunar Cycle

The lunar cycle begins with the new moon and progresses through eight major phases as the moon makes its 29.5-day journey around the Earth. Starting with the darkness and becoming more illuminated each evening, the moon reaches fullness. Then, slowly growing darker and darker, it returns to its new state to start again.

An Introduction to the Eight Phases of the Lunar Cycle   31

The New Moon   34

The Waxing Crescent Moon   38

The First Quarter Moon   41

The Waxing Gibbous Moon   42

The Full Moon   44

The Waning Gibbous Moon   49

The Last Quarter Moon   50

The Waning Crescent Moon   52

Understanding Lunar Eclipses and Blood Moons   55

Understanding Black Moons   56

Understanding Micro Moons and Super Moons   57

First Quarter Moon

Waxing Gibbous Moon

Full Moon

Waning Gibbous Moon

Last Quarter Moon

Waxing Crescent Moon

New Moon

Waning Crescent Moon

An Introduction to the Eight Phases of the Lunar Cycle

The moon completes a full orbit around the Earth in approximately 29.5 days, or one month. In fact, the word "month" comes from the word "moon." The lunar cycle begins with the new moon and progresses through eight phases as it makes its journey around the Earth. These phases reflect where the moon is in its orbit in relation to the Earth and the Sun. As the moon circles the Earth, our view of it varies depending upon how much of the Sun's light we can see reflecting off its surface.

During the time of the new moon, the moon is between the Earth and the Sun. In this phase, the moon appears dark, because the side of the moon that is reflecting the Sun's light is facing away from the Earth where we can't see it. You can think of the lighted portion of the moon as being the moon's day side and the dark part of the moon as being the moon's night side. So during the time of the new moon, only the night side is visible from Earth.

As the moon moves in a counterclockwise direction (as viewed from the northern hemisphere) around the Sun, we begin to see more and more of the moon's surface become illuminated by the Sun. These lunar phases in which the moon's light is growing are referred to as waxing. The waxing phases occur as the moon is moving from new to full; during this time the moon appears to be getting larger in the sky. This starts with the waxing crescent moon, followed by the first quarter moon, and then the waxing gibbous moon.

When the Earth is between the moon and the Sun, opposite its position during the new moon, we see this as a full moon. In this phase, the moon appears fully illuminated, because every part of the moon that is visible to us is reflecting the Sun's light. During the time of the full moon, only the moon's day side is visible from Earth. The opposite side of the moon, the side that is not visible to us on Earth, appears dark. The full moon is the only phase in which a lunar eclipse is possible because that is the only time during the lunar cycle when the Earth is between the moon and the Sun where the Earth could cast a shadow upon the moon.

As the moon continues its journey around the Sun, the lighted portion of the moon begins to decrease. All lunar phases where the moon's light is decreasing are referred to as waning. The waning phases occur as the moon is moving from full back to new. The waning phases make the moon appear to be getting smaller in the sky as less and less of the moon is illuminated by the reflected light from the Sun. The first waning phase of the lunar cycle is the waning gibbous moon, followed by the last quarter moon, and then the waning crescent moon.

Finally, the moon returns to its original place in the orbit, the new moon, where the cycle starts all over again.

The moon has a powerful effect on the Earth, from the ebb and flow of the ocean tides to its influence on menstrual cycles and sleep patterns. But this deep connection with the moon doesn't stop there. As the moon moves along on its orbital path and changes phases, the energy of the moon shifts too.

The lunar cycle is often a metaphor for what's happening in our own lives. By aligning yourself with the phases of the moon and taking note of the energies that accompany each, you'll find that things begin to flow easier. From planning to taking action, to actualizing what you desire, to reflection, you'll feel in balance with the natural rhythm of the cosmos. Rather than fighting against the current, you can choose to ride the waves of energy in the lunar cycle to create more balance and harmony for yourself and those around you. Each lunar phase brings with it certain energetic qualities, and you can use your crystals to connect with the energy of these phases more profoundly.

When is the best time to start something new, take action, or just rest and relax? It all depends on the lunar cycle. When you do this, things just seem to fall into place. Life no longer feels like a struggle because you'll finally be living in balance with the cosmos.

Just as we live out patterns in our daily lives—we wake each morning filled with energy and excitement, go about our day, and sleep each night—we live out patterns on a larger timescale. For example, if you are active all day and don't rest and recharge at night, you don't feel well and are living out of balance with your natural cycles. But by living in harmony and alignment with the phases of the moon, you can find balance between action and relaxation on a grander scale, one that fits with the way we are meant to live.

Once you understand the moon phases, you'll see how they mimic other natural cycles, like the change of seasons or the rising and setting of the Sun, and why it is so important to live in harmony with this cycle. You'll also learn how you can connect with your crystals through ritual and meditation during each phase so that you can get inspired to live in harmony and alignment with lunar energy.

The New Moon

The new moon is a time for setting goals and intentions. Working with the new moon energy each lunar cycle helps you create a commitment to yourself and to your dreams.

CORRESPONDENCES

% LIGHT 0%

CRYSTALS Black Moonstone, Golden Tiger's Eye, Rainbow Moonstone, Rhodonite

KEYWORDS adventure, anticipation, blessings, new opportunities, surprises, wishes

ENERGY

During the new moon, focus your efforts and energy on planting the seeds of things you'd like to manifest, such as better health or increased focus and creative energy. This lunar phase strongly supports the act of co-creation, so this is the time to get clear about what you want in your life. Don't get ahead of yourself by worrying about how you're going to achieve your goals. Just stay focused on the "what" and worry about taking action on the "how" later. Manifesting and intention setting can be done at any time, but by aligning to the traditional associations of the new moon phase and boosting your new moon vibes with crystal energy, you'll have a winning combination for intention setting.

Staying focused on the present moment is difficult due to the excitement of things to come, but it's imperative to set the stage for you to move forward with clarity and swift action when the time is right.

CRYSTALS

BLACK MOONSTONE Black Moonstone pairs well with the new moon because it too has a soft, dark, enveloping energy. It creates quiet mental space for you to turn your attention inward and determine what is most needed in your life. This stone is also helpful if you are struggling with attachment to the outcome of your intention. Becoming too wrapped up in whether your intention will manifest creates opportunities for doubt to creep into your mind-set. Holding space for your intention to manifest, while remaining emotionally detached, is better than worrying about the possibility of not achieving your goals. Black Moonstone helps you enjoy the journey and be present in each moment.

GOLDEN TIGER'S EYE When setting your new moon intentions, it's important to be clear about exactly what you want to invite into your life. Golden Tiger's Eye is the perfect stone for helping you get laser-focused during your new moon intention-setting ritual. It provides clarity if you're having trouble determining what's most important. Hold your Golden

Tiger's Eye in your hand, close your eyes, and ask the universe for guidance about what you should focus your energy on right now. Then just wait for the answer to present itself. Don't judge what comes through, and don't second-guess your intuition. Your higher self and the universe are working together to make sure you're on the right path—trust this!

RAINBOW MOONSTONE Rainbow Moonstone captures all the excitement of this phase and embodies the beauty of the intentions you'll set. It's representative of completion and wholeness. This crystal helps you overcome negative thought patterns or self-limiting beliefs that may creep into your head during the intention-setting process. It also enables you to understand that you're entirely and wholly deserving of manifesting the intention that you're setting for yourself. Rainbow Moonstone helps you stay in tune with the phases of the moon all cycle long—from new moon to new moon.

RHODONITE Rhodonite is especially useful for new beginnings and goal setting, so it makes for a lovely companion during this lunar phase. When you're working with Rhodonite, focus on how you want to feel. This crystal has a connection to the heart center and to the emotions, so focusing on creating a positive feeling for yourself is a powerful way to start the intention-setting process. If you can create an intention aligned with how you'd like to feel, your chances of manifesting that intention are increased exponentially because your full heart and soul will be in it!

RITUAL

Gather some paper, a pen, a black candle, a Black Moonstone, and rose-scented incense. A Rhodonite stone, a Golden Tiger's Eye stone, and/or a Rainbow Moonstone are optional.

Light the incense and the black candle. Focus on the candle flame and let your gaze soften. Pick up your Black Moonstone crystal and close your eyes.

Think about the upcoming lunar cycle and what's in store for you. If you need some inspiration, you may hold a Rhodonite stone. Think about what you'd most like to call into your life during this new moon. Ask the universe, your guides, or your higher self for clarity about your intention. Don't yet worry about how you'll accomplish this; just be open to whatever ideas flow through you. When you're ready, slowly open your eyes and set down your crystal.

What is the universe trying to tell you about the direction you should take? Use this experience to create a concise intention statement—a goal-focused affirmation—and write it down. This may be something as simple as your wish to make more time each week to meditate, or something very complex and personal to you. If you need help, hold a Golden Tiger's Eye stone for clarity and guidance.

When you've written your intention statement, pick up the Black Moonstone again and close your eyes. Visualize your intention coming to pass in as much detail as possible. Feel in your body, mind, and spirit the way you'll feel when your intention has been realized. What will your life look like and feel like once you've manifested this? If you're having trouble, you may hold a Rainbow Moonstone to help you overcome any obstacles.

Next, create an action plan for your intention by brainstorming a bulleted list of all the steps that will move you closer to your goal. What actions will you need to take to manifest it? Write these next to your intention statement.

Place your action plan on your altar and set the Black Moonstone on top as a gesture that you're planting the seed for your intention to grow. Blow out the candle and leave the list and stone in place until the full moon, when you'll switch gears from intention setting to actively manifesting.

The Waxing Crescent Moon

The waxing crescent moon is the best phase for focusing on personal development and embracing life.

CORRESPONDENCES

% LIGHT 1% to 49% lighted on the right side

CRYSTALS Green Aventurine, Green Nephrite Jade, Strawberry Moonstone, Turquoise

KEYWORDS action, expansion, manifesting, power, progress, wisdom

ENERGY

As the moon grows larger in the night sky, it acts as a metaphor for things you may wish to develop in your own life. The waxing moon is a time for progress, new experiences, and acquirement of items, skills, beliefs, knowledge, etc. This is the best time to act on the plans you made during the previous new moon. The energy of this phase supports you as you start new ventures, step into new positions, take on additional responsibilities, and embrace your personal power.

CRYSTALS

GREEN AVENTURINE Green Aventurine resonates with the energy of growth and expansion, so it's perfect for the time of the waxing crescent moon. Work with this stone when you want to add a little cosmic fertilizer to the intention seeds you planted during the previous new moon.

GREEN NEPHRITE JADE This stone of wealth and good luck pairs well with the waxing crescent moon's manifesting properties. It encourages deep thought and enhances wisdom, so it's helpful if you're feeling unsure about how to take action on your new moon plans.

STRAWBERRY MOONSTONE This little-known Moonstone has a pale vermillion color. It encourages you to get to work on the action plan you created during the previous new moon. Hold this stone or carry it in your pocket when you need a motivational boost.

TURQUOISE Turquoise is a stone of ancient wisdom that instills patience. It enhances your ability to think things through before rushing forward if the path ahead is still unclear. Work with this stone if you need to take time to find clarity and fill any gaps in your knowledge before making rash decisions.

During a **waxing crescent moon**, sit in front of your new moon action plan, still
with the Black Moonstone atop the paper, and hover your hands above it. Feel the energy
of your intention and visualize yourself completing the steps on your checklist.
Add a Green Aventurine stone, representing the expansion of this energy,
atop the paper next to the Black Moonstone.

Find a quiet space in nature during a *first quarter moon* and settle in with a White Moonstone. Set your stone on the earth and visualize it filling up with energy. Pick up the stone, hold it above your head, and visualize it glowing with universal light. Now hold the stone over your heart and celebrate everything you've accomplished in this lunar cycle so far.

The First Quarter Moon

The time of the first quarter moon is best used to release outworn belief systems and patterns that are no longer for your highest good.

CORRESPONDENCES

% LIGHT 50% light on the right side

CRYSTALS Angelite, Carnelian, Rose Quartz, White Moonstone

KEYWORDS bravery, communication, love, obstacles, romance, wellness

ENERGY

This is a time for new things, so get rid of the people, ideas, and things that aren't serving you well. Get creative during this releasing process, and strive for clear communication with others as you make the transition. Don't be afraid to request support from your friends and family.

CRYSTALS

ANGELITE Angelite assists with clear communication and works to share with others while you're shedding old patterns and beliefs. The baggage you're releasing right now will weigh you down if you don't let go of it. It could stop you from manifesting your intentions, so use your voice to ask for support, patience, and healing when needed.

CARNELIAN Work with Carnelian during the time of the first quarter moon to keep yourself motivated and on track with your new moon action plan. If you feel yourself starting to lose steam, take some time to soak up some good Carnelian vibes.

ROSE QUARTZ This crystal helps you get honest with yourself about the people and things that are holding you back from reaching your true potential. You may not want to admit to some of these, but Rose Quartz's gentle support helps you face the truth with an open heart and mind.

WHITE MOONSTONE This common Moonstone variety reinforces the progress you've made up to this point in the lunar cycle. You're one-quarter of the way through this lunation, so there's still a lot to experience, but you're well on your way to creating positive life transformation.

The Waxing Gibbous Moon

Take time to celebrate your little wins and achievements during this lunar cycle.

CORRESPONDENCES

% LIGHT 51% to 99% light on the right side

CRYSTALS Blue Lace Agate, Citrine, Coffee Moonstone, Snowflake Obsidian

KEYWORDS acceptance, celebration, discernment, jubilation, surrender, tranquility

ENERGY

It's all too easy to get caught outside of present moment consciousness by always looking toward the future. For example, if you've set a goal or intention to lose ten pounds, celebrate each and every pound you lose rather than waiting until you've hit your final goal. Instead of waiting for life's big moments, use the waxing gibbous phase to hold space for joy and the recognition of your present accomplishments. It's almost time to manifest the intentions you've set during the new moon, so relax into the moment and allow things to unfold.

CRYSTALS

BLUE LACE AGATE Blue Lace Agate is a stone of hope and joy. Work with it to help you celebrate the small steps you've taken toward creating a happier life. This crystal reminds you to be present in the moment, releasing pain from the past or anxiety about the future, so that you're able to enjoy the here and now.

CITRINE This golden variety of Quartz is known for its powerful manifesting ability. Because the full moon—the peak time for manifestation—is fast approaching, it's time to turn things over to the universe and let the energy of the cosmos take it from here. With Citrine by your side, you'll add a little extra magic to your wishes for this lunar phase.

COFFEE MOONSTONE This earthy brown Moonstone helps you relax and appreciate the calm moments leading up to the full moon. The waxing gibbous moon is about surrendering and letting things take shape. You've done your part to manifest new things into your life; now it's time to let Spirit take the reins.

SNOWFLAKE OBSIDIAN Snowflake Obsidian is about balance. You've just gone through an intense period of action; now you're moving into a period of rest. Take time to appreciate the place of balance between these.

Visit your favorite body of water during a **waxing gibbous moon**. This could be a river, a pond, a lake, or the ocean (or even a fountain). Hold a Citrine and visualize your intention coming to pass. Fill the stone with positive energy and then toss it into the water, signaling that you've done your part and are now turning it over to the universe for assistance.

The Full Moon

It's time to reap the rewards of the seeds you planted during the new moon!

CORRESPONDENCES

% LIGHT 100% lighted

CRYSTALS Amethyst, Labradorite, Rainbow Moonstone, White Moonstone

KEYWORDS achievement, completion, dreams, flow, intuition, manifestation, power, protection, wholeness

ENERGY

This is the peak time to engage your intuition and use your psychic gifts, such as clairvoyance or clairaudience, so be on the lookout for any signs or symbols that present themselves in your life. For example, do you keep seeing a specific number? Have you come across an animal messenger? These may be signs from the universe. The energy of the full moon is incredibly powerful, so be gentle with yourself and allow yourself to be fully immersed in this energy. Go with the flow rather than fighting what is being revealed. Allow sensations of wholeness and completion to wash over you as your dreams are manifested into being.

Although manifesting usually takes center stage during the time of the full moon, there's another important aspect to its energy that shouldn't be overlooked. The bright light of the full moon illuminates things that may otherwise be hidden to you and calls your attention to potential roadblocks or challenges that, if left unchecked, can slow down your progress. This isn't to say these things must come to pass, only that if you remain on the present path, they could be issues. Luckily, the full moon is also known for its protective qualities, so a little ritual and some course corrections can head off any potential troubles.

Finally, the full moon is a powerful time for divination work. Because your intuition is heightened during this period, you'll feel more connected to your divination practice, and the results will show it.

CRYSTALS

AMETHYST People have been using Amethyst to connect with intuition and psychic skills since the time of the ancient Romans. Incorporate Amethyst into your full moon divination practice for ease in deciphering the messages and information you receive. Alternatively, call upon Amethyst's protective abilities and charge your crystal with full moon energy to create a powerful protection talisman.

LABRADORITE Labradorite is a mystical stone that gets its brilliant flash from reflected light, similarly to how the full moon is illuminated by reflected light from the Sun. The energy of Labradorite and the energy of the full moon are like kindred spirits. Work with them together to enhance any full moon rituals or activities. You can also use Labradorite during this moon phase to facilitate lucid dreaming and to promote insightful, intuitive dreams. Tuck a piece of Labradorite into your pillowcase or create a simple rectangular grid using four pieces around your bed to have an out-of-this-world dream experience.

RAINBOW MOONSTONE Believe it or not, Rainbow Moonstone is a white variety of Labradorite. They're the same stone, but where Labradorite has flashes of color on a dark, gray-colored crystal, Rainbow Moonstone has flashed of color on a light, white-colored stone. Rainbow Moonstone works similarly to Labradorite for dreamwork, but it also encourages you to stay in flow with the lunar cycle all year long. Some people tend to notice the moon only when it's full, but they miss out on the true benefits of living in tune with the moon. Work with Rainbow Moonstone to cultivate a lasting lunar practice that will serve you all cycle long.

WHITE MOONSTONE White Moonstone is a member of the Orthoclase Feldspar group of minerals, different than Rainbow Moonstone (which is actually a member of the Labradorite Feldspar group). With its soft, white shimmer, it was named for its resemblance to the moon.

This crystal mimics the energy of wholeness and completion embodied by the full moon. If you feel like something has been missing from your life, wear or carry White Moonstone to draw it to you. This crystal has a dynamic, feminine, receptive energy that makes it great for manifesting what you desire.

RITUAL

Because the full moon is a time of heightened intuition and enhanced psychic skills, one of the best ways to connect with its energy through ritual is by using cartomancy. Cartomancy is the ancient art of card reading divination. Tarot and Lenormand are some of the most popular historical systems of card reading, but many modern mystics and intuitives use oracle cards as well.

Try this eight-card spread on the evening of the full moon to provide insight into the time between this full moon and the next. You can repeat this reading each full moon for a look at the month ahead.

Start by shuffling a deck of your favorite oracle cards. Place eight cards in a circle, starting at the twelve o'clock position and moving clockwise until you have pulled eight cards. Use the meaning of the card positions below to put the symbols, words, and imagery from each card into context.

CARD 1 – NEW MOON This card represents new beginnings and new opportunities that are on the horizon.

CARD 2 – WAXING CRESCENT MOON This card represents things that you're actively manifesting into your life right now.

CARD 3 – FIRST QUARTER MOON This card represents things that need to be communicated, especially things related to your relationships.

CARD 4 – WAXING GIBBOUS MOON This card gives advice about things to consider when making an important upcoming decision.

CARD 5 – FULL MOON This card reveals things you know to be true intuitively, but that you may be ignoring or reluctant to admit.

CARD 6 – WANING GIBBOUS MOON This card is a reminder of things you may need to reflect on at this time.

CARD 7 – LAST QUARTER MOON This card shows you areas in your life where you would benefit from more independence.

CARD 8 – WANING CRESCENT MOON This card represents things that need to be released from your life before you can move forward.

To banish a negative or jealous person from your life during a **_waning gibbous moon_**, place a Black Obsidian stone in a small pouch with some dried barley or caraway seed. Keep your pouch near a window. Any time you need to set firm boundaries with the person who is pushing your limits, hold the pouch while speaking their name.

The Waning Gibbous Moon

During this moon phase, reflect on what you've just manifested into your life during the full moon.

CORRESPONDENCES

% LIGHT 51% to 99% light on the left side

CRYSTALS Adularia, Aquamarine, Black Obsidian, Lapis Lazuli

KEYWORDS boundaries, destiny, letting go, receiving, reflection, rumination

ENERGY

The waning gibbous moon is also known as the Disseminating Moon. You've just brought new energies and experiences into your life during the period of the full moon. Get ready to continue to receive the residual blessings that are flowing to you, and prepare for what is still yet to be manifested. Know that everything happens in divine timing, and accept what is happening as part of the universe's plan for you as a spiritual being.

CRYSTALS

ADULARIA Adularia is a gemmy variety of Moonstone that promotes inner reflection and recapitulation. The stone itself has a shimmering, reflective surface and reminds you to turn inward as the moon shrinks back toward darkness.

AQUAMARINE Aquamarine holds the energy of water and works well with the waning gibbous moon because it helps unexpected blessings wash up on your shore. It's a stone of receiving, and it allows you to embrace your worthiness of the gifts the universe still has in store for you.

BLACK OBSIDIAN Black Obsidian helps you create boundaries where they are needed. As blessings continue to flow your way after the time of the full moon, you may be bombarded with people looking to drain your energy or those who harbor jealousy about the positive things you've created in your life. This crystal keeps them at bay, compassionately but with firm protective boundaries.

LAPIS LAZULI Lapis Lazuli has been used for magical workings since ancient times. It's strongly aligned with destiny and soul path work. Reach for this stone if you need some support or help understanding what is, or is not, being sent to you from the universe.

The Last Quarter Moon

During the last quarter moon, it's time to dig deep
within yourself and find your inner strength.

CORRESPONDENCES

% LIGHT 50% light on the left side

CRYSTALS Clear Quartz, Peach Moonstone,
Pyrite, Rhodochrosite

KEYWORDS compassion, epiphany,
independence, oneness, solitude, strength

ENERGY

The last quarter moon is also known as the
Third Quarter Moon. This is a time to reflect
on your mind-set and your inner world. In the
previous moon phase, the waning gibbous
moon, you worked on release and detachment;
now you need to turn away from the outside
world altogether and focus on yourself.

Embrace this solitude and independence while
remaining heart-centered, compassionate, and
filled with empathy. Although you're focused on
the self at this time, it's important to remember
that you're part of the greater whole. Part of
your self-discovery is recognizing that we are
all connected; we are all one.

CRYSTALS

CLEAR QUARTZ Clear Quartz instills a
clarity of mind that can result in an important
epiphany about your role in the world and what
you're meant to do to walk your soul path.

PEACH MOONSTONE This feminine-
energy stone has a receptive, intuitive quality
that makes it a natural partner for the time
of the last quarter moon. As the lunar cycle is
drawing nearer to completion, there's often a
desire to retreat inward and spend time alone.
Enjoy this solitude and the quiet moments
it provides.

PYRITE This masculine-energy crystal
balances the energy of Peach Moonstone,
while still allowing you to honor your desire for
space and time alone. In fact, it complements
this natural behavior by encouraging you to be
independent and self-reliant, at least during
the time of the last quarter moon.

RHODOCHROSITE Rhodochrosite helps
you tune into the wavelength of love and
compassion all around you and experience
a sense of oneness with others, even when
you're physically separate from them.

Go somewhere you can be alone for little while during a *last quarter moon*. Place a Peach Moonstone in your feminine (nondominant) hand and a Pyrite in your masculine (dominant) hand. Feel energy flow into your receiving hand, move through your body, and exit out of your sending hand. As the energy continues to loop, you become balanced and aligned with the energy of the last quarter moon.

The Waning Crescent Moon

During the waning crescent moon phase, you continue your inward retreat
by diving deep into your emotional landscape.

CORRESPONDENCES

% LIGHT 1% to 49% light on the left side

CRYSTALS Apricot Botswana Agate, Black Moonstone, Blue Calcite, Tangerine Moonstone

KEYWORDS emotions, release, relaxation, rest, solitude, stillness

ENERGY

The waning crescent moon is also known as the Balsamic Moon. It's the last phase in the lunar cycle before it begins again. This is a time to feel fully and deeply. Prepare to plan new things with passion during the next phase by storing up your energy reserves now. It's also your last chance to release anything that's been hanging on in your energy field during this lunar cycle before moving into the new cycle with the coming new moon. Take time to clear your slate for a fresh start before the end of the lunar cycle.

CRYSTALS

APRICOT BOTSWANA AGATE This crystal corresponds to the Sacral Chakra, and it is deeply tied to creativity and the emotions. Apricot Botswana Agate helps you tap into your emotional center so that you can release anything that's stuck in your energy field, especially energies that are slowing down your progress.

BLACK MOONSTONE The very last part of the waning crescent moon, the time just before the new moon, is known as the Dark Moon. Use Black Moonstone to connect with this energy and take one last chance for rest and rejuvenation before the next lunar cycle. Retreat into the darkness so that you can emerge refreshed and full of energy.

BLUE CALCITE This crystal promotes relaxation and helps you feel comfortable with the stillness. If you struggle with quiet moments and feel the need to fill every second with thought or activity, reach for a Blue Calcite stone to help you find comfort in the silence.

TANGERINE MOONSTONE Work with this stone to start building up your energy reserves for the next lunar cycle. It fills up your energy body with good vibes.

During a **waning crescent moon**, cut a sheet of paper into small rectangles and write something you'd like to release on each piece. Place the pieces of paper in a bag. Hold an Apricot Botswana Agate in your hand and pull a slip of paper from the bag. Read it and then place the paper and the stone over the area of your Sacral Chakra. Exhale while intending to release any stagnant energy related to this issue.

Understanding Lunar Eclipses and Blood Moons

Full lunar eclipses occur when the Earth is directly between the Sun and the moon and it casts a shadow on the moon's surface. For this to happen, the moon must be in the full moon position, so full lunar eclipses can only occur when the moon is full. Because full lunar eclipses happen during the full moon phase, but the moon appears dark from the Earth's shadow, they contain the energies of both the full moon and the new moon together. This spectacular phenomenon only lasts for a few hours, but it's a very powerful time to work with lunar energy.

Some full lunar eclipses are called Blood Moons (not to be confused with the October Blood Moon of the thirteen modern moons; see page 120 for more on that). A Blood Moon lunar eclipse occurs when the light from the Sun passes around the edges of the Earth, through part of the Earth's atmosphere. It can cast a reddish color onto the moon, depending upon the weather, particulates present in the atmosphere, and several other variables.

Blood Moon eclipses aren't common, so when they do occur it's a wonderful experience to be able to work with their energy. The Blood Moon eclipse is an incredibly magical event; taking time for deep spiritual practice during this eclipse can be very powerful. Perform a ritual or ceremony, meditate, create something artistic, or celebrate with loved ones. However you choose to align yourself with the energy of the Blood Moon eclipse, remember to celebrate life itself. The Blood Moon eclipse reminds you of the blood that gives you life, that is flowing through your veins. This is a special time to practice gratitude and show your thanks for the life you have. Treat this cosmic event with respect and reverence, and enjoy the special energy that will only come along a handful of times in your lifetime.

Understanding Black Moons

A Black Moon is traditionally defined as the second new moon (or Dark Moon) in a given calendar month. However, there are several other lunar events that are referred to as Black Moons, which can make things a bit confusing.

Some modern Pagans use the term "Black Moon" to refer to a month without a full moon. The only month in which this is possible is February: Because a full lunar cycle takes approximately 29.5 days to complete, and February usually only has 28 days (or 29 days in a leap year), then from time to time, depending on the previous full moon date, the month of February may be missing its full moon.

Additionally, the term "Black Moon" is used by some modern Pagans to refer to the second full moon in a given month to avoid confusion with the dual meaning of the term Blue Moon (as discussed in "Understanding the Blue Moons" on page 98). However, this has led to further confusion with our original definition of the term, the second new moon in a month.

If you come across a reference to a Black Moon, you need to get some context about which type of Black Moon is being discussed. Alternatively, if a date is given, you can consult a lunar calendar to determine the type of Black Moon being referenced. Learning to read and interpret a lunar calendar is an invaluable skill to have at your disposal. There are many excellent paper moon calendars published annually, and there are more than enough phone-based apps and websites to make checking the moon phase of any given date simple.

Understanding Micro Moons and Super Moons

It seems that anyone who is even a tiny bit familiar with astrology has heard of a Super Moon. People seem to get quite excited when a Super Moon makes an appearance. But what exactly is a Super Moon?

The term "Super Moon" is used to describe the moon when it's at its closest orbital point to the Earth. The true astronomical terminology for this moon is the perigee full moon, or if you want to get technical, it's the "perigee syzygy of the Earth Moon Sun system." The word *perigee* is the astrological term for the moon's closest orbital point to the Earth, and the word *syzygy* refers to the occurrence of three or more astral bodies in alignment.

The Super Moon may get your attention because it's quite a bit brighter—some sources say nearly 30 percent—than an average full moon. However, this extra reflected light is still just barely noticeable to most people.

Although the Super Moon is as close as possible to the Earth, there is only a very slight increase in its apparent size (it appears about 7 percent larger). Again, this difference isn't really enough to be noticeable. However, tons of people claim to have seen the Super Moon looking like a giant in the sky. How can this be? It has to do more with the moon's position in relation to the horizon than its position at perigee. When the moon rises and sets—whenever it's closer to the Earth's horizon—it appears larger. But this is true every night, not just on the eve of a Super Moon.

The lesser-known Micro Moon, also called Mini Moon, is the opposite of a Super Moon. During a Micro Moon, the moon is at its orbital point farthest from Earth. This is known as the apogee full moon.

CHAPTER 3

Crystals for the Lunar Zodiac

As the moon travels around the Earth, it passes through the twelve Zodiac constellations. While in each sign, it takes on that sign's energetic qualities. Thus, because the moon has such a strong influence over us, the Lunar Zodiac plays an important role in shaping the cosmic energies that affect our day-to-day experiences.

An Introduction to the Lunar Zodiac	60
The Aries Moon	65
The Taurus Moon	66
The Gemini Moon	69
The Cancer Moon	71
The Leo Moon	73
The Virgo Moon	74
The Libra Moon	77
The Scorpio Moon	79
The Sagittarius Moon	80
The Capricorn Moon	83
The Aquarius Moon	84
The Pisces Moon	86

An Introduction to the Lunar Zodiac

The night sky can be divided into twelve sections, one relating to each constellation of the Zodiac—a set of twelve constellations surrounding the Earth and moon. As the moon travels around the Earth, it passes through the sections of each Zodiac constellation. This is referred to as "entering" or being "in" a particular Zodiac sign. Because the moon makes its rotation around the Earth pretty quickly, in just about twenty-nine days, it moves into a new sign every two to three days.

When the moon enters a specific sign, it takes on the energetic qualities of that sign. Astrologers use those qualities to create lunar forecasts describing what to expect as the moon enters each sign. The moon has a strong influence over us, given that it's our nearest celestial neighbor, so the Lunar Zodiac is vital to explaining the cosmic energies that shape our experiences. For example, if the moon is entering Leo, key themes and energies may include courage and strength— Leo's qualities. But if the moon is entering Gemini, communication and joy will be of greater consideration and influence.

Because the moon moves through each sign so rapidly, the energies of each Zodiac sign never stick around for long. So if there are some signs you find particularly challenging, there's no need to panic. Tracking these energies and using them to your advantage for crystal or ritual work can prove quite helpful. Let's say you are calling in more abundance. It would be beneficial to do this work when the moon is in the signs of Virgo (career) or Scorpio (magnetism and resourcefulness), whereas it may be more difficult to find success when the moon is in the signs of Cancer (emotions) or Leo (drama).

MOON PHASES AND THE LUNAR ZODIAC

In addition to the energy of the Lunar Zodiac, consider the current moon phase as the moon moves through the sky. The lunar phase changes the way in which the qualities of a Zodiac sign's energy will manifest in your life. You'll need to take it into account for a more complete understanding and accurate description of the current energetic influences of the moon. Getting a good moon calendar (one that shows both lunar phases and astrological signs) will help you determine when energies will be joining together.

For example, a new moon in Cancer has a different energy than a full moon in Cancer. A new moon in Cancer combines the Cancer Moon's associations with emotions, empathy, family, imagination, peace, and tenacity with the new moon's connection to fresh starts, surprises, new opportunities, and positive experiences. You may expect that a new moon in Cancer would prompt positive emotional experiences, new opportunities born of tenacity and hard work, new beginnings that create peace and end turmoil, or surprises related to family matters such as marriage or birth announcements.

A full moon in Cancer, however, combines the same associations with emotions, empathy, family, imagination, peace, and tenacity with the full moon's connection to intuition, achievement, and wholeness. A full moon in Cancer may prompt your intuition to enhance your feelings of empathy and provide insight into the emotions of others. It may see your whole family coming together in celebration, or it might mean that your tenacity and dedication will result in an important life achievement.

You can see from this example that the moon phase vastly alters how we experience the energetic qualities of the Lunar Zodiac. Interpreting these energetic combinations may seem difficult, but it gets easier with practice.

YOUR MOON SIGN

When considering the astrology of the moon and its energetic effect on your life, it's important to think about the sign the moon is currently in, but you should also consider your moon sign for a complete picture of how the moon's energy will affect you on a personal level. You may be familiar with your sun sign, the sign the Sun was in when you were born, because it is commonly used for horoscopes and astrological predictions. Your sun sign is related to your conscious mind and dictates your outward personality and ego self. However, your moon sign has a great effect on how you relate to astrological influences from the cosmos and the world around you as well.

Your moon sign is the sign the moon was in when you were born. It is the inner part of you that's more sensitive and emotional. It's related to your subconscious mind and vulnerabilities, and it dictates what you need to feel safe and secure in the world.

Remember, the moon moves into a new sign at a fairly rapid pace, changing signs every two to three days. This means that although you may share the same sun sign as another person, you may be vastly different types of people if your moon sign is different. Even if you share the same outward personality, the core personal needs that lie beneath—and that are the driving force behind the ego—may be quite varied. This ultimately changes the way your sun sign is expressed.

Additionally, this is the reason that some people never feel their horoscopes are accurate. Horoscopes are generally written based on broad assumptions about people's sun signs. If you're often left disappointed reading the predictions based on your sun sign, try reading the horoscope that's linked to your moon sign instead to see whether it shines some light on what's going on internally.

YOUR MOON SIGN AND THE LUNAR ZODIAC

You should also consider how your individual moon sign may interact with the moon when it's in certain Zodiac signs. Understanding how these energies work together can give you a clearer picture about your own personal strengths and weaknesses and how the moon's energy may affect you personally.

For example, a person with a Taurus moon sign will have a different experience when the moon is in Cancer than a person with a Sagittarius moon sign. A person with a Taurus moon sign would put the Cancer Moon's associations with emotions, empathy, family, imagination, peace, and tenacity into context for them personally by relating those qualities to the Taurus Moon's connection to devotion, intellect, love, persistence, reliability, and responsibility. You may expect this person to experience devotion to family, work hard to fulfill responsibilities, let their love of others enhance feelings of empathy and compassion, or use their intellect to fuel their imagination, possibly by inventing something new, writing music, or teaching others.

A person with a Sagittarius moon sign, however, would relate the same associations with emotions, empathy, family, imagination, peace, and tenacity to the Sagittarius Moon's connection to generosity, goals, honesty, inspiration, passion, and travel. You may expect this person to feel the needs of others and give generously to assist them, set goals and quickly achieve them, bare their soul to family in a moment of emotional honesty, let their imagination inspire new thoughts and ideas related to their hobbies, or find peace and soul-level satisfaction through travel during the time of the Cancer Moon.

If you're struggling with self-worth issues, take a minute during the time of the *Aries Moon* to write down some of your most common negative thoughts about yourself on a small piece of paper. It may feel painful to see these things on paper, but this is part of the process of recognizing just how damaging it is to be carrying these thoughts around with you. Place a lit candle in a fireproof container and carefully burn the paper containing your negative self-thoughts. Intend to release these from your mind and energy body. Hold a Ruby crystal and think of one affirmation to replace each negative thought that was released. Carry the Ruby with you as a reminder of the positive self-image you are cultivating. Repeat this exercise as needed.

The Aries Moon

When the moon is in Aries, you may find yourself preoccupied with what others think about you.

CRYSTALS Lava Rock, Red Garnet, Ruby

DATES March 21 – April 19

ELEMENT Fire

KEYWORDS courage, determination, honesty, leadership, strength, willpower

RULING PLANET Mars

Even if you consider yourself to be a pretty grounded person, your self-image may suddenly feel important to you when the moon enters Aries. This could be because you've suddenly found yourself in the spotlight and feel pressure to put your best foot forward. However, it may also be caused by unchecked self-confidence struggles or self-worth issues that are rearing their heads during this time, when you should instead be focused on courage and inner strength. Not to worry: with the right crystals and mind-set, you can banish the negativity that's dragging you down.

LAVA ROCK Lava Rock aligns well with the energy of the Aries Moon. It provides a much-needed boost of self-confidence, especially in group settings. It also encourages you to feel comfortable in your own skin. This stone helps you draw on your inner strength to take control of any negative thoughts that are affecting your self-worth.

RED GARNET This crystal is associated with courage and bravery. If you've been letting your ego-mind run wild with thoughts about how you stack up to others, reach for a Red Garnet to help you ditch the comparisons. People often compare themselves to others they know or admire as a way of seeing how they fit into society and what role they fill. Red Garnet encourages you to be brave and just be yourself.

RUBY This red variety of Corundum is filled with fire and passion. It helps you overcome mind-set blocks that may be keeping you from recognizing your true worth. This is especially true for those in leadership positions or for people who find themselves thrust into the spotlight. Ruby burns up negative self-thinking and helps you shine your inner light.

The Taurus Moon

During the time of the Taurus Moon, focus on self-love.

———

CRYSTALS Apache Tear, Pink Opal, Rose Quartz

DATES April 20 – May 20

ELEMENT Earth

KEYWORDS devotion, intellect, love, persistence, reliability, responsibility

RULING PLANET Venus

Self-love during the Taurus Moon can mean daily self-care or big picture care-taking. It is also a good time to focus on your financial well-being. Start by scheduling time for self-care. This can be as simple as getting yourself a green juice, or it may be something more elaborate such as a spa day. This is also an important time to take stock of your security and finances. Is your current financial situation supporting you? If so, how can you continue on this path? If not, what changes can you make to improve it? When you feel secure, it allows your body, mind, and spirit to relax and feel supported. If you don't have a stable foundation in place, make it part of your self-care practice to take steps toward changing this situation.

APACHE TEAR This stone makes a perfect partner for the nurturing energy of the Taurus Moon. It has been used to support those who are grieving or suffering from a broken heart, but it can also be applied to grieving lost parts of the self. If you haven't been caring for yourself, or if you always put the needs of others above your own, Apache Tear can help you reclaim your sacred self-care time.

PINK OPAL This is the ultimate stone for instilling compassion and empathy. If you struggle with taking time for self-love, or don't feel deserving of it, reach for a Pink Opal stone. It helps you hold compassion for others, and for yourself as well.

ROSE QUARTZ Rose Quartz is connected to Venus, the ruling planet of Taurus. This crystal exudes love and helps you take time to nurture yourself. The Taurus Moon is a great time to add a few extra minutes to your morning routine for a cup of herbal tea, or pencil in a day for painting or gardening to nourish your spirit.

During the *Taurus Moon*, draw yourself a hot bath and add a few tumbled Rose Quartz stones and some dried chamomile flowers (or a few fresh rose petals) to the water. Ease yourself into the tub and hover your hands above the water. Envision a pink light, filled with love energy, coming from your heart into the water. Visualize the water glowing pink, and see the Rose Quartz stones filled with pink light. Bathe your body with the water and feel the waves of love pour over you as it touches your skin. Remain in the bath as long as you'd like.

To create a *Gemini Moon* crystal wand, arrange a few small Blue Apatite and Howlite stones or beads along the length of a natural Selenite wand. Attach them with jeweler's glue or copper wire following the product instructions. Hold your wand in your hands, close your eyes, and place it over your Third Eye Chakra parallel to your spine. Allow the energy of the wand to open you to new experiences and the positive life lessons that await you. Make a mental note of any symbols, words, or images that you see, as they may be important to your journey.

The Gemini Moon

The Gemini Moon is related to learning and new experiences. This is fueled by curiosity and the desire for greater understanding.

CRYSTALS Blue Apatite, Howlite, Selenite

DATES May 21 – June 21

ELEMENT Air

KEYWORDS adaptability, communication, cooperation, curiosity, joy, kindness

RULING PLANET Mercury

Often, the knowledge gained during the Gemini Moon provides valuable lessons that will soon be needed in life. The Gemini Moon also encourages you to be flexible and adapt to new situations. Satisfying your curiosity often requires you to have new experiences or meet new people. This may be difficult for introverts, but the energy of Gemini's ruling planet, Mercury, can give you the encouragement you need to try something new. You'll likely be glad for the experience, and you'll look back at what you've accomplished with pride and joy.

BLUE APATITE This crystal encourages you to explore the world around you, either physically through travel, or intellectually through learning new things and expanding your knowledge base. Blue Apatite gives you a gentle nudge to step just outside of your comfort zone, while helping you remain in the moment so you don't miss out on the present experience by dwelling on the past or worrying about the future.

HOWLITE Howlite challenges your beliefs about the world and your role in it. It supports you while encouraging you to be flexible in your thinking. Pair it with Blue Apatite to help you keep an open mind during new adventures and experiences.

SELENITE This high vibrational stone is an excellent protector. Work with it to draw in universal white light to shield and protect you. After connecting with the supportive energy of Selenite, you'll feel more confident during the new experiences you face during the Gemini Moon. Additionally, this crystal helps expand your conscious awareness so that you're better able to understand and integrate the universal lessons being shared with you at this time.

During the time of the *Cancer Moon*, place a Larimar stone in the center of the room with your home's main entrance. Sit down, make yourself comfortable, and close your eyes. Feel the energy of the room. Does it lift you up or drag you down? Open your eyes and look around. What do you notice that could use a little love and attention? Write down your feelings and observations about the space, and at least three things that could be done to improve the energy or aesthetics of this room. Move to the next room, and repeat. Once you've gone through your entire home, choose three tasks from your list to complete during this Cancer Moon.

The Cancer Moon

When the moon is in Cancer, your home and family life take center stage.

CRYSTALS Angelite, Larimar, Rainbow Moonstone

DATES June 22 – July 23

ELEMENT Water

KEYWORDS emotions, empathy, family, imagination, peace, tenacity

RULING PLANET Moon

It's all too easy to take home and family for granted, but making your family members feel appreciated can go a long way toward improving family relationships, especially during the time of the Cancer Moon. Spend time doing some of your favorite family activities, or catch up on the list of things that need to be done around your house. Take it a step further than doing your regular house chores and give your home some TLC. Repair anything that's broken, replace things that are worn out, or even liven things up with a fresh coat of paint! Putting some positive energy into your home moves you into alignment with the energy of the Cancer Moon, and the good vibes you create will stick around for many moons to come.

ANGELITE Work with Angelite to call upon your angels and guides to protect your family and home space. This crystal is connected to the water and air elements, so it helps you tap into your intuition and emotions simultaneously. Take advantage of this powerful energetic combination by tuning into how others feel so you can support them. Supporting those you love during this time makes things at home feel balanced and harmonious.

LARIMAR This blue variety of Pectolite is aligned with the watery energy of the Cancer Moon. Work with it to wash away, both physically and energetically, anything that no longer feels positive or supportive in your home. Your inner energy reflects your outer environment, so allow Larimar to guide you as you improve your space.

RAINBOW MOONSTONE A favorite of many healers and lightworkers, Rainbow Moonstone can be used during the time of the Cancer Moon to enhance your intuition and psychic skills.

Set a Danburite crystal outside or on a windowsill under the light of the *Leo Moon* to absorb as much of this creative, passionate Leo energy as possible. Block out some time for creative expression through art, dancing, cooking, gardening, or any other form you choose. Pick up the charged Danburite crystal and hold it over your Sacral Chakra for about a minute. Breathe deeply. Then, move the stone to the area of your Solar Plexus Chakra and repeat this deep breathing. Feel yourself filled with the energy of the Leo Moon and feel it boost your creativity. End your time by holding the Danburite crystal over your Heart Chakra and send your gratitude to the stone for the energy it has shared with you.

The Leo Moon

During the Leo Moon, take time for things that bring you pleasure.

CRYSTALS Danburite, Fire Agate, Golden Tiger's Eye

DATES July 24 – August 23

ELEMENT Fire

KEYWORDS courage, creativity, drama, generosity, persuasion, strength

RULING PLANET Sun

The key to enjoying the energy of the Leo Moon is to live with passion. You may want to do something romantic and spontaneous for your partner or express your passion by focusing on your hobbies or activities. Leo is ruled by the Sun, the planetary body connected with creativity, so this is a great time to try things that showcase your artistic talents, such as painting, singing, playing music, dancing, cooking, or baking. Follow your heart and let passion be your muse. The things you create at the time of the Leo Moon are channeled through you from the universe.

DANBURITE This crystal captures the energy of the Sun, Leo's ruling planet. Danburite encourages you to live in the moment and enjoy life. It also nudges you to share your own inner light through creative expression. No matter what type of artistic expression you choose, Danburite allows you to create from a place of authenticity and higher consciousness.

FIRE AGATE This stone gets its name from the ember-like flashes of light on its surface. It resonates with the fire element and makes a great companion for the Leo Moon. Fire Agate encourages you to find new ways to express romantic feelings or passion for your partner. Think outside the box rather than resorting to the same old gestures. Your creativity and spontaneity will be well received by your partner. Make a grand gesture to show how you feel.

GOLDEN TIGER'S EYE This crystal embodies confidence and inner strength, both of which are useful when diving into your hobbies with vigor. How do you most enjoy spending your time? Golden Tiger's Eye encourages you to do more of these things during the time of the Leo Moon.

The Virgo Moon

When the moon is in Virgo, you'll feel at ease by keeping things orderly and organized.

CRYSTALS Emerald, Green Aventurine, Moss Agate

DATES August 24 – September 22

ELEMENT Earth

KEYWORDS career, dedication, determination, health, intellect, loyalty

RULING PLANET Mercury

During the Virgo Moon, stay on top of to-do lists and chores to keep things running smoothly and avoid obstacles. Pay attention to your routines and schedules and be sure you stick to them. If you're having a difficult time, don't be afraid to ask for help from family or coworkers. This is also a time to check in on your physical health. How are you feeling? Take this time to evaluate what will bring you back into balance.

EMERALD It's all too easy to get swept up in your own thoughts during this time, but Emerald gently reminds you to get out of your head and into your heart every once in a while. Work with Emerald if you feel your mind buzzing with activity and need a moment of stillness. This crystal also reminds you to check in with your feelings before acting or making big decisions.

GREEN AVENTURINE This stone encourages practicality, something that Virgo's ruling planet, Mercury, demands during this time. Organization, schedules, and routines are important during the Virgo Moon, but not if they overcomplicate things. Green Aventurine helps you be mindful about what's helping you be more successful and what's just getting in the way.

MOSS AGATE This earthy stone is a favorite for physical healing. Work with Moss Agate to put the Virgo Moon energy to good use by creating a new workout routine, meditation practice, or weekly meal plan. If you feel like you don't have time or energy to care for your physical body, Moss Agate helps you make it a priority. With the energy of the Virgo Moon supporting you, it feels easy to start new, healthy habits.

During the time of the *Virgo Moon*, light a green candle, pick up a Moss Agate stone, watch the candle flame, and start to think about your physical body. What can you do to improve your health? Do you need to eat better? Exercise more? Have more quiet time? Add energy healing or massage to your routine? When you're ready, write down a list of things you'd like to do to nourish your body. Then, hold an Emerald crystal while you transfer your list into your calendar; schedule these activities—big and small—now so that you hold space for them in your routine.

This exercise will show you how others view your role in the world. During the time of the *Libra Moon*, trace the outline of a bowl onto a piece of paper to create a circle. Cut it out and draw lines dividing it into eight equal sections. Use colored pencils to shade each section a different color. Label the sections with one of the following archetypes: Artist, Dreamer, Fool, Healer, Leader, Scholar, Servant, and Warrior. Cast (gently drop) three tumbled Rainbow Fluorite stones onto the circle. Make note of the archetype on each area where a stone lands. If a stone falls outside of the circle, disregard it. If a stone falls on the line between two areas, note both archetypes. Take a moment to contemplate what these archetypes mean and whether these are roles that you'd like to fill. Will you conform or rebel?

The Libra Moon

When the moon is in Libra, be mindful of your interactions with others.

CRYSTALS Azurite, Blue Sapphire, Rainbow Fluorite

DATES September 23 – October 22

ELEMENT Air

KEYWORDS cooperation, grace, harmony, imagination, justice, partnership

RULING PLANET Venus

The time when the moon is in Libra is important for relationships of all kinds, from friends and family, to acquaintances and coworkers, or even those with whom you have a difficult time seeing eye to eye. The opposing energies of competition and cooperation are at odds, and how you engage with others will influence the outcome of each interaction. Cooperation is always more pleasant and productive than competition, so try to keep your relationships working in your favor.

AZURITE This deep indigo stone is connected to the Third Eye Chakra and stimulates creative expression and the imagination. Work with this crystal when you need a little intuitive help understanding the thoughts or feelings of others. When you can put yourself in someone else's shoes (or their head, for that matter), it's easier to hold compassion for them and work in cooperation.

BLUE SAPPHIRE This crystal promotes peace and harmony, especially among groups of people. If you've been dealing with a tumultuous situation, Blue Sapphire can help you remove your ego from the equation, set your differences aside, and find some common ground with others.

RAINBOW FLUORITE Rainbow Fluorite promotes clear thinking and allows you to see what's most important in any situation. If you've been feeling scattered or pulled in lots of different directions, work with this crystal to get back on track. It can also bring clarity to your role in projects, relationships, or social groups, and help you better understand what people expect from you. However, this doesn't mean you need to agree with these roles. Whether you choose to conform or rebel against these societal expectations, Rainbow Fluorite will guide you on your path.

During the time of the *Scorpio Moon*, light a gold candle with the intention of calling in prosperity and abundance. Place a coin in your receiving (nondominant hand) and a Jet stone in your sending (dominant) hand. The coin represents the money that comes to you, while the Jet represents the money that you spend. Notice how you're holding your hands. If you're holding your earning hand lower, it means you likely earn and save more abundance than you spend, but if you're holding your spending hand lower, you may be spending out of alignment with what you're currently receiving. It's important to find balance between earning, spending, and saving. Look into the candle flame and feel your hands naturally move back into balance. Repeat this any time you need to bring your finances back into alignment.

The Scorpio Moon

During the Scorpio Moon, transformation and change one on the horizon, especially relating to finances and relationships.

CRYSTALS Black Obsidian, Black Opal, Jet

DATES October 23 – November 22

ELEMENT Water

KEYWORDS intuition, magnetism, passion, resourcefulness, trust, truth

RULING PLANET Mars

Be mindful of maintaining balance between your income and debt, as well as between yourself and your romantic partner, during the Scorpio Moon. Giving and receiving must happen equally to maintain a happy partnership. You should also be aware of gossip and secrets during this time.

BLACK OBSIDIAN Obsidian is a stone of mystery, so it pairs perfectly with the energy of the Scorpio Moon. Scorpio energy is often misunderstood; if you've had miscommunications during the Scorpio Moon in the past, work with Black Obsidian. This crystal helps you avoid hurt feelings by communicating with others clearly and concisely. It also helps reveal people's true intentions, gossip, or secrets that may cause problems if left undiscovered.

BLACK OPAL Black Opal is full of brilliant, colorful flecks set on a dark backdrop. If you have hit a rough patch in your romantic life, Black Opal helps you rediscover happiness in your relationship. However, it can also reveal deeper issues that may be present in your romantic partnerships. It offers you an objective look at what this partnership means for you so that you can determine the best road forward. Black Opal works with the energy of the Scorpio Moon to show you where your partnership is out of balance so that you can address it and work on it together.

JET Jet encourages you to get realistic about your finances. Are your earnings, spending, and savings in alignment? How can you create positive change in this area of your life? Working with Jet can help you see important factors you may have overlooked in the past.

The Sagittarius Moon

During the time of the Sagittarius Moon, focus your attention on bettering yourself through education.

CRYSTALS Citrine, Imperial Topaz, Lapis Lazuli

DATES November 23 – December 21

ELEMENT Fire

KEYWORDS generosity, goals, honesty, inspiration, passion, travel

RULING PLANET Jupiter

Take time to learn new things, especially related to philosophy, history, geography, or religion and spirituality, during the Sagittarius Moon. These will benefit you in the future in ways you cannot possibly imagine. This is a great time to travel or to make travel plans, as seeing and experiencing the world helps broaden your horizons even more than traditional education can. Pay attention to your dreams, as they will impart deep wisdom and share important messages with you. Finally, use some of this time for spiritual exploration through ceremony, ritual, meditation, or any other method to which you feel drawn.

CITRINE Citrine sparks your intellect and encourages you to stimulate your mental body with new ideas, deep conversations, and philosophical questions about the nature of consciousness and your role in the universe. This is the perfect companion stone when you're learning new things about yourself and the world around you.

IMPERIAL TOPAZ This golden to peach variety of Topaz is prized for its color and relative rarity. It is one of the traditional Sagittarius Zodiac stones and can bring you into alignment with the energy of this moon. Imperial Topaz can enhance ceremony and ritual work as well as help you connect with your ancestors and call upon them for any wisdom and guidance that may be needed at this time.

LAPIS LAZULI Jupiter is the ruling planet of Sagittarius and has a strong tie to Lapis Lazuli. Work with Lapis when you're ready to branch out and explore the world. This crystal promotes adventure and travel, and it encourages you to embrace your wanderlust.

On the evening of the *Sagittarius Moon*, make yourself comfortable where you can see the light of the moon. Light your favorite incense as an offering to your ancestor spirits. Place a medium-size ceramic or porcelain bowl of water where you can see the moonlight reflecting off its surface. Gently drop an Imperial Topaz crystal into the water and watch the movement of the ripples on its surface. When the movement has slowed, attempt scrying into the water. Look for signs, symbols, or messages that your ancestors may share with you. If you don't see anything, soften your gaze, let your eyes go in and out of focus, and try again. Sit in meditation until the incense burns completely.

During the *Capricorn Moon*, choose a Capricorn crystal for this meditation: Buddstone if your goals and tasks are clear but you need a little energetic support to begin; Rainforest Jasper if you'd like help staying focused so you can get back on track with your soul's calling; or Smoky Quartz if you're ready to use your natural talents to serve others, but you need clarity on the best route to take. Hold the stone over the area of your Root Chakra, close your eyes, and breathe deeply for a few moments. Visualize the energy of the stone expanding outward and filling your Root Chakra with its energy. Ask the universe and the energy of the Capricorn Moon for assistance in reaching your goals.

The Capricorn Moon

When the moon is in Capricorn, it's time to buckle down and work on projects that require leadership and focus.

CRYSTALS Buddstone, Rainforest Jasper, Smoky Quartz

DATES December 22 – January 20

ELEMENT Earth

KEYWORDS ambition, bravery, discipline, grounding, loyalty, responsibility

RULING PLANET Saturn

It's important to move forward toward your goals with everything you've got during the Capricorn Moon. This time is especially auspicious for all things related to your career or business. Alternatively, this may be the time to focus on the legacy you'll leave in this world. What do you want to be known for? How do you want to make positive change in the world and be of service? The Capricorn Moon can help you find clarity to answer these questions as well as take action to share your gifts with the world.

BUDDSTONE The energy of this stone feeds your ambition and enhances your excitement about achieving your goals. It increases your vitality and gives you the energy you need to see your projects through so you can reap the rewards of your hard work and focus.

RAINFOREST JASPER This earthy crystal keeps you grounded while you tackle the task at hand. If you tend to get distracted or lose focus, take advantage of the energy of the Capricorn Moon to complete important projects. Rainforest Jasper is connected to both the Root Chakra and the Heart Chakra, so it supports your business and career goals, especially those aligned with your soul path and things you love doing.

SMOKY QUARTZ Smoky Quartz is well known for its grounding abilities, so it pairs perfectly with the moon while it's in Capricorn. Work with this crystal if you're ready to make big life changes that will better align with your soul path so that you can be of service to others in the way that suits you best and makes use of your natural talents.

The Aquarius Moon

When the moon's in Aquarius, let your joyful, sunny personality shine through.

CRYSTALS Blue Fluorite, Blue Lace Agate, Celestite

DATES January 21 – February 19

ELEMENT Air

KEYWORDS communication, compassion, freedom, friendship, logic, wit

RULING PLANET Uranus

A warm smile can inspire others into action and lift up those in need, especially during the Aquarius Moon. Friends are important during this period, so take time to reach out to loved ones to catch up. Don't let the busy Capricorn Moon energy spill over into Aquarius, or your friends and family may feel neglected. Nurture your relationships and show others how much you care about them. Communication is an ever-present theme during the Aquarius Moon, so if you do feel the need to spend time wrapping up projects you started during the Capricorn Moon, put your energy toward networking and fostering relationships that will further those plans.

BLUE FLUORITE This air element stone helps clear your mind so that communication comes easily. It helps you choose just the right words, even in difficult conversations when you need to tread carefully with what you say. It has a joyful energy that keep things light and allows you to lift up others with your words.

BLUE LACE AGATE This lovely stone promotes hope and optimism. It opens the Throat Chakra and allows you to speak clearly and with purpose. It also enhances group harmony and cooperation, so it's the perfect crystal to keep in your pocket or handbag for get-togethers with family and friends during the time of the Aquarius Moon. It's an excellent stone for building relationships, so don't be shy about meeting new people and growing your network of friends and colleagues when you're working with this crystal.

CELESTITE Work with Celestite to call upon advice and assistance from your angels or spirit guides. It relates to the air element and enhances communication between you and helpful celestial beings.

During the *Aquarius Moon*, make yourself comfortable in your sacred space and light a stick of your favorite incense. The smoke represents air; it carries your thoughts and your words into the universe. Hold a piece of Celestite over your Throat Chakra, or lay down and set it gently on your throat. Think about a statement or question you'd like to communicate to your angels or spirit guides. Speak this aloud or think it quietly to yourself and visualize the incense smoke carrying its energy to your guides. See the energy moving outward into your space, leaving through the ceiling, and traveling up into the sky. Close your eyes and visualize it continuing to travel out into the universe, through the cosmos, until it reaches your guides. Take some deep breaths in and out. Quiet your mind, and listen for a reply. Sit in meditation until the incense is gone.

The Pisces Moon

At the time of the Pisces Moon, it's important to turn inward and focus on your spirituality.

—

CRYSTALS Amazonite, Aqua Aura Quartz, Larimar

DATES February 20 – March 20

ELEMENT Water

KEYWORDS creativity, compassion, intuition, kindness, romance, wellness

RULING PLANET Neptune

While the moon was in the last house of Aquarius, communication with others was key, but as the energy shifts into Pisces, you'll find inner reflection and soul searching to be most rewarding. The water element plays an important role during this time, heightening both your emotions and your intuition. This can be productive for air, water, and earth signs, or for those who are very in tune with their intuition, but fire signs may find this period challenging, as it often brings their shadow sides to the surface.

AMAZONITE This stone carries the energy of the water and air elements and helps you tap into your emotions as a source of strength. Amazonite assists with releasing stagnant emotional energy that's blocking you from reaching new levels of spiritual consciousness.

Work with this crystal to let go of things that no longer serve you. This crystal helps you remain patient, compassionate, and full of self-love if you do encounter any shadow side issues during the Aquarius Moon.

AQUA AURA QUARTZ This stone is an intense emotional balancer (in a good way!). If you've been letting the Aquarius vibes take you on an emotional roller coaster, this crystal helps you regain control of the situation and mellow things out. It's not about dulling your feelings, though; instead, it's about choosing to feel in a way that lifts you up. Only you have the power to choose how you feel.

LARIMAR This gem, known as the Dolphin Stone, helps you ride the energetic waves of the Aquarius Moon with poise. It enhances your intuition, so reach for this stone if you need universal guidance.

During the *Pisces Moon*, set a dish of water in your sacred space and gently place an Amazonite stone into it. Place a second Amazonite crystal just in front of the dish. Dip your finger in the water and rub a drop or two over your Heart Chakra and Third Eye Chakra. Close your eyes and feel the energy of the crystalline water energizing the two chakra centers. Take a deep breath in, and as you exhale, visualize breathing out any negative or stagnant emotional energy. See this energy move toward the water, where it can be transmuted into positivity. Continue this process until all the negative emotional energy has been released. Now visualize the second Amazonite stone glowing brightly with positive energy. On your next inhalation, see yourself breathe in this light until your aura is full of new, positively charged energy.

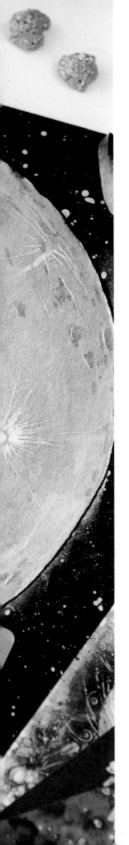

CHAPTER 4

The 13 Full Moons of the Year

People from around the world have been naming the full moons of the year since ancient times. In almost all cultures and civilizations, the moon was used to track seasonal events, from hunting, gathering, and farming to important holidays and celebrations. Following the light of the moon throughout the year allowed our ancestors to anticipate the season's coming tasks and record the passage of time.

An Introduction to the 13 Full Moons of the Year   90

The 13 Modern Moons   92

The 13 Native Moons   95

The 13 Celtic Moons   97

Understanding Blue Moons   98

An Introduction to the 13 Full Moons of the Year

Since long ago, people from cultures and traditions around the Earth have been naming the full moons of the year. Some groups had as few as four of five moon names (given for the major seasons), while others had twelve (one for each calendar month) or thirteen (one for each lunar month). The names were often applied not just to the moon itself, but to the entire month in which that moon occurred.

Early American settlers and many Native American tribes, for example, used moon names to track important seasonal events. Native peoples were already using this system when settlers arrived in North America from Europe. When the settlers learned of this system, they began using it for themselves, with adapted names better suited to the activities and holidays that they were accustomed to. For example, the Native Fish Moon was changed to the Growing Moon because the settlers relied more upon agriculture than they did fishing. The Celtic, Chinese, European, Germanic, and Hindu peoples also had their own moon names, and in fact, moon names are still being used today by many followers of Earth-based spiritual traditions.

Historically, full moons were given names that described animals and nature, agricultural tasks, the weather in a given region, or important happenings in that moon month, observed by the cultures that named them. These moon names helped people track the seasons and the important activities that allowed them to live in harmony with nature. Names that described which animals and game to hunt, which crops to sow or harvest, probable weather or seasonal changes, the stages of raising livestock, and local celebrations or holidays allowed people to follow the cycles of these important activities from year to year. This was also a way for early people to record the passage of time. Tracking the seasonal moon names served as a type of calendar where no formal calendar was used.

There were also times when the moon names would change from one year to the next to serve as a historical record as well as a calendar. For example, the month of the Harvest Moon may fluctuate from year to year. The Harvest Moon is the moon closest to the Autumnal Equinox. This occurs most frequently in September, but a few times per decade it occurs in October instead. If this happens, then the October Moon claims the name Harvest Moon and the September Moon is named for the main crop being harvested.

With moons being named by many different cultural groups, hailing from different parts of the globe, dealing with differences in climate, and practicing different ways of life, the names themselves became incredibly varied. Some groups shared the same name for the same moon month. Others used the same name to describe different moons depending on variables such as weather. For example, for Native groups in northern climates, the name Snow Moon may have been given to a month as early as November, whereas Native peoples in the south may have used the same name to refer to the month of January, because that's when snow may have begun to arrive.

The names listed for the moons in the following sections of this book have been applied to the twelve months of the Gregorian calendar, because it is the calendar used most commonly in the world today. Every effort has been made to maintain the historical integrity of these names and what they represent, but at times they needed to be simplified to fit within the context of a twelve-month calendar. That means you can time the given rituals with the appropriate full moons of the year. Because three variations (modern, Native, and Celtic) have been presented for each month of the year, you'll be able to choose the tradition, crystals, or ritual that you feel most connected to.

The 13 Modern Moons

The thirteen modern moons in this book were collected from a wide range of rich cultural and historical traditions, from ancient to modern. They are referred to here as the "modern" moons not because they originated in modern times, but because these names are still commonly in use today. In most instances, the main moon name given is the modern Pagan or American settler name, and the listed alternative names come from Chinese, Greek, Roman, or Germanic Anglo-Saxon (Old English) names for the moons.

As you read about the modern moons, pay attention to how each moon got its name and consider its importance to those who named it. The modern crystal moon rituals have been adapted from both traditional and modern practices for connecting with lunar energy. They incorporate magical items and deities that correspond to the cultures that gave these moons their names.

By adopting a global view of different ways to come into balance and alignment with the moon, you'll be able to see the common threads that bind all of humanity. As you practice these monthly rituals, open yourself to the experiences that these varied cultural traditions have to offer. This will help you gain a deeper understanding of just how important the moon was (and still is!) to people from around the world.

When working with these moons in your own way, feel free to incorporate any deities or magical items that inspire a connection to the energy of each moon. Consider the keywords associated with each moon and what they mean to you in your own life; then call upon your favorite god or goddess, herb, or essential oil to support you in coming into alignment with that energy.

The 13 Native Moons

The thirteen Native Moons in this book are by far the most difficult to describe. With so many different Native tribes, cultural traditions, and important stories, finding common threads is not always easy. In most instances, the main moon name given is the most commonly used name among the Algonquin tribes, and the listed alternative names come from other well-known tribal peoples from North America, Central America, and South America.

The crystal moon rituals in this section have been created using common modern ritual practices that draw inspiration from the traditional plant and animal medicines of many Native American cultures. Every effort has been made to respect and honor the traditions and heritages of these tribes while also allowing for creativity and inspiration to guide a modern approach to ritual work with these energies.

As you read about the Native Moons, put yourself in the shoes of those who lived in harmony with the natural cycles. Consider the lessons from the deities and totem animals that can be applied to present-day life. What are the commonalities between yourself and the tribal peoples who were some of the first in the world to name the moons each month? What is different in your own life compared to the lives of those who gave these moons their names? What wisdom can you take away from recognizing those differences?

When working with the lunar rituals for the Native Moons, push yourself to find new ways to incorporate the corresponding totem animals and healing herbs into your ritual. Remember, your ritual may be as simple or as complex as you like. The point is to create a moment of sacredness between you and the moon, so listen to your inner guidance for how to customize each ritual to meet your needs.

The 13 Celtic Moons

The thirteen Celtic Moons in this book are compiled from ancient and modern approaches to Celtic magic, including Druidism. The Druids, a scholarly and spiritual group of Celts, were best known for their magic, healing abilities, and knowledge. Although not much is known about the Druids, they play an important role in the modern interest in Celtic spirituality, including the Neo-Druidism movement. The main moon names for the Celtic Moon months are from the Neo-Pagan Celtic tree calendar, which is said to be derived from the Ogham alphabet system. The Ogham was an alphabet based on trees, and it was used to write an early form of the Irish language.

Although its authenticity is debated by some scholars, the Celtic tree calendar can be used quite effectively to correspond to the energies of the thirteen moons of the year and map the changing of the seasons. While the Ogham tree alphabet wasn't likely used by the Celts as a calendar, many modern spiritual practitioners have found it to be a very fulfilling way to connect with lunar energy, even if this tradition isn't rooted in sound historical research.

Similarly to the calendar adaptation of some of the characters of the Ogham, the twelve major monthly trees (excluding the blue Ivy Moon) have been used to create a modern Celtic astrological Zodiac system. Again, its authenticity is hotly debated by scholars of Irish history (and rightfully so!). It is often referred to as the Celtic Tree Zodiac, Celtic Astrology, or Irish Astrology and has gained popularity in recent years. The Celtic Tree Zodiac can be applied to lunar energy in a way that is similar to how the Western Zodiac can (see chapter 3). Just don't get too caught up in the origin of this system, as there's not much historical research to support its use further back than just a few decades ago.

Understanding Blue Moons

Each of the four seasons—spring, summer, autumn, and winter—lasts three months, filling the days between the solstices and equinoxes (totaling twelve months in a calendar year). Given that the lunar cycle lasts about 29 days, this would mean that there's usually only one moon per month, or three per season. But because the length of a calendar month doesn't exactly match up with the length of a lunar cycle, there will occasionally be an extra, fourth, moon within the same season. The third of these moons in a four-moon season is traditionally known as a Blue Moon. This would occur only once every nineteen years or so.

However, in 1946, an article by James Hugh Pruett titled "Once in a Blue Moon" was published in the March issue of *Sky & Telescope Magazine*. In this article, the author identified a Blue Moon as a second full moon within a calendar month. In this instance, the first full moon in a month would go by its monthly moon name, and the second would be called the Blue Moon. This form of Blue Moon occurs about every two and a half to three years and can only happen if the first full moon takes place within the first three days of the calendar month.

Finally, others refer to a Blue Moon as the thirteenth moon in a given calendar year for years when there are thirteen full moons rather than twelve.

Additionally, the term Black Moon has been used by modern Pagans to refer to the second full moon in a given month to avoid confusion with the dual meaning of the term Blue Moon. However, this in itself has led to some confusion, as the second new moon in a month can also be referred to as a Blue Moon. Some modern Pagans identify the Blue Moon with the Crone aspect of the Triple Goddess.

CHAPTER 5

Crystals for the 13 Modern Moons

The thirteen modern moons described in this section have their roots in a variety of cultural traditions and historical periods. What they all have in common, however, is that all these names are still in use today. Whether attributed to modern Pagans, American settlers, the people of China, or the ancient Greek, Roman, or Germanic peoples, these moon names have endured through from their origins until modern times. Their connection to tradition and the cycles of nature has kept them relevant throughout the ages.

January: The Wolf Moon	103
February: The Ice Moon	104
March: The Storm Moon	107
April: The Growing Moon	109
May: The Hare Moon	110
June: The Rose Moon	112
July: The Hay Moon	115
August: The Corn Moon	116
September: The Harvest Moon	119
October: The Blood Moon	120
November: The Snow Moon	123
December: The Cold Moon	124
Blue: The Blue Moon	126

To connect with the energy of the **Wolf Moon**, place one of the crystals (Labradorite, Selenite, or Black Moonstone) on your altar or in your sacred space near an illustration or a statue of one of the dark goddesses (Hekate, Baba Yaga, or Kali). Meditate in the presence of the stone while holding the intention to transition into the new year with ease.

JANUARY
The Wolf Moon

The Wolf Moon is named because it occurs during a time when wolves howled more than usual, out of hunger, because food was scarce. The sound of their howling was especially loud in the crisp, winter air. The alternative name, Disting Moon, is from a festival from the Middle Ages. This feast was held on the first full moon of the Runic calendar and prepared people for the return of the spring season.

ALTERNATE NAMES Disting Moon, Holiday Moon, Moon After Yule, Moon When Wolves Run Together, Winter Moon

ANIMALS falcon, owl, wolf

COLORS black, gray, white

CRYSTALS Black Moonstone, Labradorite, Selenite

DEITIES Baba Yaga, Hekate, Kali

ESSENTIAL OILS cedar, cypress, pine

HERBS juniper, meadowsweet, vervain

KEYWORDS communication, rebirth, solitude

BLACK MOONSTONE Black Moonstone is connected to the idea of new beginnings and is perfect to work with during the time of the Wolf Moon, the first full moon of the year. Black Moonstone is linked with the dark goddesses Hekate, Baba Yaga, and Kali. These goddesses are often feared because of their perceived negative connotations, but in fact, they represent transformation. Black Moonstone assists you during times of uncomfortable change as both an emotional and an energetic support.

LABRADORITE Wolves have long been revered as mystical creatures, so Labradorite, a highly magical stone, is aligned with the wolf totem. Wolves need freedom to be content. In your own life, Labradorite can provide a spiritual freedom that may otherwise be difficult to obtain. This stone also connects you with the deep wisdom and magic of the goddesses Hekate, Baba Yaga, and Kali.

SELENITE Selenite is a bringer of light, so it is needed at this very dark time of the year. This crystal helps shine some light on the path that's before you as you embark on the new adventure that awaits you.

The Ice Moon

The Ice Moon occurs during the intense cold. The Germanic name for this moon is the Horning Moon because it's the time when reindeer begin shedding their yearly antlers. It's also known as the Quickening Moon because it appears just before spring, when time seems to quicken up and bulbs begin to push their way through the soil toward the sun. This is a time for planting the seeds of hope for good things to come.

ALTERNATE NAMES Budding Moon, Candles Moon, Horning Moon, Quickening Moon, Sage Moon, Wild Moon

ANIMALS bear, eagle, white fox

COLORS blue, purple, white

CRYSTALS Amethyst, Clear Quartz, Rose Quartz

DEITIES Aphrodite, Aquilon, Artemis, Diana, Eros, Khione

ESSENTIAL OILS palma rosa, primrose, sage

HERBS hyssop, orange mint, Saint John's wort

KEYWORDS clarity, intuition, perception

AMETHYST Amethyst is a stone of intuition. Work with it to bring clarity to intuitive messages. When paired with Clear Quartz, Amethyst helps you see what you've overlooked and provides guidance for the next steps on your journey. Be prepared!

This stone also reveals aspects of your shadow side that you've been failing to acknowledge, but these challenging aspects of your personality can become strong allies when used to your advantage.

CLEAR QUARTZ Clear Quartz elicits unmatched mental clarity. Work with this stone to identify things that are no longer serving you that need to be released. This crystal helps you set intentions for what you'd like to call into your life to fill the void from the things you'll leave behind.

ROSE QUARTZ Rose Quartz invokes the energy of Aphrodite and encourages you to take time for self-love during this last period of rest before spring. Use tumbled Rose Quartz in your bathwater to immerse yourself in the loving energy of this goddess, or wear Rose Quartz jewelry for peace and to promote self-care.

To connect with the energy of the *Ice Moon*, place a Clear Quartz crystal atop a picture of Artemis or Diana and ask for guidance or clarity about anything that has been troubling you or weighing heavily on your mind. This goddess will help guide your thoughts, like an arrow toward its target, to exactly what you need to hear.

To connect with the energy of the *Storm Moon*, place a Pink Tourmaline crystal in a jar of water overnight to charge the water with energy. Sow some seeds from your favorite type of herb (or start them indoors if you're in a colder climate). Remove the stone from the jar and water the seeds while thinking of all that you're grateful for.

MARCH
The Storm Moon

The Storm Moon is named because heavy rains occur this time of year, signifying the arrival of spring. Christian settlers knew this moon under the name Lenten Moon, while the Anglo-Saxons referred to it as Hraed Monath (Rugged Month Moon) or as Hlyd Monath (Stormy Month Moon). It was also known by early settlers as the Seed Moon because it indicated that the time for sowing seeds had begun. Some modern-day Pagans call it the Death Moon, as it signifies the fading away of the winter months, making way for the newness of spring.

ALTERNATE NAMES Death Moon, Hlyd Monath Moon, Hraed Monath Moon, Lenten Moon, Plough Moon, Seed Moon

ANIMALS boar, horse, lion

COLORS lavender, purple, white

CRYSTALS Amethyst, Lodestone, Pink Tourmaline

DEITIES Aphrodite, Astarte, Astoreth, Black Isis, Cybele, Ishtar

ESSENTIAL OILS jasmine, magnolia, violet

HERBS catnip, lavender, sage

KEYWORDS balance, passion, transformation

AMETHYST The energy of the changing seasons can feel overwhelming as slow-paced winter comes to an end and the Earth begins to awaken. Amethyst helps you work through turbulent and transformative energies. Making this crystal your companion helps you harness this energy and put it to good use, rather than letting it sweep you up in a whirlwind of overwhelm.

LODESTONE Lodestone attracts what you need most. Work with Lodestone and the goddesses Aphrodite, Astarte, Astoreth, or Ishtar to call in a mate (or to rekindle passion with your current partner). Alternatively, use it to invoke Athena and call in wisdom and knowledge that will bring you new life experiences and circumstances.

PINK TOURMALINE It's important to maintain a sense of peace and stability this month. Work with Pink Tourmaline as part of your gratitude practice and take time to hold space for all the things you're thankful for in your life. Focusing on gratitude will plant the seeds for more goodness to manifest in your life.

To connect with the energy of the *Growing Moon*, journal for three to five minutes about a project you'd like to begin. Make lists, draw doodles, and express your hopes about this project. Then fold the paper in half and draw a beautiful tree on the outside. Place a Chrysoprase stone on the paper and hold space for your project to grow. Keep this in a place where you'll see it often until your project is complete.

The Growing Moon

The Growing Moon is so named because it occurs when things have begun to sprout: seeds are germinating, trees begin to leaf out, and bulbs push out from the earth. The Medieval English called this the Budding Trees Moon. Additionally, some modern Pagans know this moon as the Awakening Moon because it is associated with the return of the Maiden after the time of the Crone.

ALTERNATE NAMES Awakening Moon, Budding Trees Moon, Grass Moon, Maiden Moon, Planter's Moon, Waking Moon

ANIMALS ant, heron, monkey

COLORS blue, green, red

CRYSTALS Blue Calcite, Chrysoprase, Green Nephrite Jade

DEITIES Anahita, Blue Tara, Gaia, Hathor, Herne, Ma'at

ESSENTIAL OILS dragon's blood, geranium, patchouli

HERBS basil, chamomile, chives

KEYWORDS expansion, growth, rejuvenation

BLUE CALCITE Blue Calcite has a soft, gentle energy that nurtures all life. It is strongly connected to the maternal Egyptian goddess Hathor. Learn to care for yourself and others as you would a tender seedling with the help of this crystal. It is loving, yet firm, helping you create necessary boundaries where they are lacking in your life (especially when they relate to your emotional well-being).

CHRYSOPRASE This feminine stone carries the vibrational energy of love from Mother Gaia. It is intrinsically linked to care of the Earth's flora and fauna. Work with this stone any time you'll be working with plants or animals. This crystal also inspires hope to grow within you as it relates to projects you're creating and nurturing in your life.

GREEN NEPHRITE JADE Jade has long been associated with luck, health, and well-being. Its green color is associated with growth and healing. This stone has been known to enhance the growth of plants and is perfect when used during the time of the Growing Moon to grid your herb or vegetable garden.

MAY

The Hare Moon

The Hare Moon is so named because it's the time when the weather is warm enough for the hares to be seen in abundance. In Roman mythology, the hare is a sacred animal associated with the spring season. Additionally, May gets its name from the Greek goddess of motherhood, Maia, and some Europeans refer to this moon as the Mothers' Moon.

ALTERNATE NAMES Buddha Purnima Moon, Dragon Moon, Merry Moon, Mothers' Moon, Vesak Moon

ANIMALS duck, hare, hen chick

COLORS brown, green, yellow

CRYSTALS Emerald, Rhodonite, Rose Quartz

DEITIES Astarte, Cybele, Isis, Maia, Priapus, Rhea

ESSENTIAL OILS copal, grapefruit, honeysuckle

HERBS borage, lovage, sweet woodruff

KEYWORDS action, beauty, fertility

EMERALD Emerald is the traditional May birthstone, but it also has associations with fertility and abundance, which make it the perfect stone to use during the time of the Hare Moon. It is strongly linked to mother goddesses such as Astarte, Cybele, and Rhea, as well as fertility deities such as Priapus. Work with Emerald to embody fertility energy, either physically or as a metaphor for creativity and birthing new ideas.

RHODONITE This stone features bold, black lines across a pink background. Its appearance is a metaphor for the balance between tenderness and sternness that we need to learn important life lessons. We are all faced with an abundance of decisions and lessons that shape the people we become. Sometimes these lessons are gentle and other times they are tough, but both together help create who we are. Work with Rhodonite when you're beginning something new or are faced with an important decision.

ROSE QUARTZ This stone is a symbol of beauty and is connected to Isis. Legends say that Isis had a beauty ritual where she would gather tumbled Rose Quartz stones from the Nile River. She would massage her face with the cool stones to enhance her appearance.

To connect with the energy of the *Hare Moon*, place a tumbled Rose Quartz stone in a bowl of ice water until it's cool. Remove the stone from the water and gently rub it over your face, starting at the top and working your way down. Feel free to use your favorite facial oil and follow with a rose toner mist.

The Rose Moon

The Rose Moon was named by European-American settlers for the rose flower, which blooms at this time. June was named for the Roman goddess of marriage, Juno, and this moon is also known as the Lovers' Moon (because many people have June weddings). It is also known as the Honey Moon, because honey begins production this month. In fact, the term "honeymoon" got its name from the sweet period after a wedding that lasts about a month (or one moon) long. The name Dyad Moon is the moon nearest the Summer Solstice, when day and night are of equal length. (*Dyad* refers to something being made of two parts.)

ALTERNATE NAMES Bright Moon, Dyad Moon, Honey Moon, Lovers' Moon, Mead Moon, Strong Sun Moon

ANIMALS bee, luna moth, sparrow

COLORS gold, light blue, yellow

CRYSTALS Citrine, Honey Calcite, Rose Quartz

DEITIES Apollo, Helios, Ra, Sol, Surya, Usil

ESSENTIAL OILS chamomile, lotus, rose

HERBS dock, mullein, yarrow

KEYWORDS beauty, connection, love

CITRINE This crystal is known for its mood-boosting qualities and ability to help manifest what you need. It's connected to sun deities such as Apollo, Helios, Ra, Sol, Surya, and Usil. Work with Citrine to balance your chakra centers and bring the light of the Sun into your energy field.

HONEY CALCITE Gaze into a piece of Honey Calcite and appreciate the moments that create the sweetness of life. Honey Calcite evokes the positive energy of summer. This crystal is full of dancing rainbows and joyfully reconnects you to the world around you.

ROSE QUARTZ Rose Quartz is a gentle Quartz stone that has been tinged with rosy color. This stone of love, passion, compassion, friendship, and empathy is perfectly suited to the time of the Rose Moon because it enhances marriage and love of all types (romantic, friends, family, divine, etc.). Allow love to pour over you every time you connect with this crystal.

To connect with the energy of the *Rose Moon*, place a single rose flower (red, pink, or white) in the farthest right corner of your home. In feng shui, this area relates to love and relationships. Place a Rose Quartz crystal next to the flower to charge it with energy. Allow the flower to dry, and sprinkle the petals in your next bath.

To connect with the energy of the *Hay Moon*, fill a drawstring pouch with dried mugwort or valerian herbs. Place a Rutilated Quartz stone inside the pouch and tie it closed. Hold the pouch in your hands on the night of the Hay Moon and ask for guidance to come to you in your dreams. Tuck the pouch in your pillowcase and go to sleep.

JULY

The Hay Moon

The Hay Moon is so named because it corresponds to the time when hay is harvested from the fields. The Anglo-Saxon name for this moon is the Wort (Wyrt) Moon because it occurs when the worts—herbs and medicinal plants— were harvested for drying and preservation.

ALTERNATE NAMES Blessing Moon, Hungry Ghost Moon, Meadow Moon, Summer Moon, Wort Moon, Wyrt Moon

ANIMALS deer, jackal, mouse

COLORS gold, green, orange

CRYSTALS Apricot Moonstone, Fire Opal, Rutilated Quartz

DEITIES Athena, Diana, Janus, Nephthys, Pan, Venus

ESSENTIAL OILS lemon verbena, rose geranium, sage

HERBS lemon balm, mugwort, valerian

KEYWORDS healing, motivation, mystery

APRICOT MOONSTONE This stone helps you manifest what you desire using your creative energy. Apricot Moonstone connects to the Sacral Chakra, the center for birthing new ideas into being. It helps you gather energy from the universe to support your dreams and desires. This stone works especially well when kept with you from the time of new moon intention setting until the evening of the Hay Moon.

FIRE OPAL This special variety of Opal is unlike any other, with its vibrant yellow to orange color and green fire. It's an excellent pick-me-up during the hottest days of the summer and motivates you to get through important tasks or chores without feeling exhausted.

RUTILATED QUARTZ The fine, golden needles within this stone look like straws of hay. These golden Rutile crystals are also thought to resemble fine golden hair, so this stone is also known as Venus Hair Quartz, after the Roman goddess of love and beauty. This stone is an excellent healer, as it breaks up and removes energetic blockages so that energy can flow more freely throughout the body. It makes the perfect companion during the Hay Moon because it prepares the physical body for healing by bringing the energy body back into balance.

The Corn Moon

The Corn Moon is so named because it occurs at the time when corn begins to be harvested. Additionally, it is known as the Dog Days Moon because it shared the night sky with Sirius, the dog star.

ALTERNATE NAMES Dog Days Moon, Lynx Moon

ANIMALS dog, lynx, quail

COLORS peach, red, yellow

CRYSTALS Carnelian, Peach Aventurine, Yellow Sapphire

DEITIES Hathor, Hekate, Mars, Nemesis, Thoth, Vulcan

ESSENTIAL OILS chamomile, lemongrass, rosemary

HERBS cedar, rue, tulsi

KEYWORDS karma, pleasure, reflection

CARNELIAN This deep orange stone nourishes you by pulling energy into your energy field (called your aura). Just as we sustain the physical body by enjoying the results of a bountiful harvest, so too must we nourish the energy body. The Corn Moon is about enjoying the fruits of your labor due to the effort you've put in previously. Carnelian helps you do this in your own life by encouraging joyful activities related to the Sacral Chakra (such as creativity, dancing, or sex). Taking part in these pleasurable activities helps recharge your energy body.

PEACH AVENTURINE This stone has a tender energy that instills gratitude. Let it fill your heart with grateful thoughts while the buzzing energy of summer slows and the seasons shift into a time of calm and inner reflection. Peach Aventurine will help you keep kindness and generosity top of mind during the time of the Corn Moon.

YELLOW SAPPHIRE These small, golden stones look similar to corn kernels. Like the corn seed, they hold the potential for returning your energy back to you a hundredfold when tended and cared for. Make a Yellow Sapphire crystal your companion during times of spiritual growth to enhance your journey and receive the fullness of the gifts the universe is prepared to offer you.

To connect with the energy of the *Corn Moon*, write a desire you have about the future of your spiritual journey on a corn husk. Use the husk to wrap a tumbled Carnelian stone and some dried, loose cedar in a bundle. You may need to tie the bundle with a string. When you're ready to call in this spiritual energy, open the bundle and burn the cedar while holding the crystal.

To connect with the energy of the *Harvest Moon*, fill a small basket with symbols of the harvest—such as apples and other fresh fruit, colorful leaves, squash or gourds, and grains—as well as a few coins. Finally, add a Citrine, Jade, or Orange Calcite crystal while focusing your intention on nourishing your body, mind, and spirit. Feel gratitude for all the blessings in your life. Display the basket in a place you'll see it often and eat a piece of the fruit each time you need to boost your gratitude.

The Harvest Moon

The Harvest Moon occurs at the time of the fall harvest. The light of this full moon allows farmers to work all night to finish harvesting crops. Another name for this moon is the Singing Moon, because people would sing in celebration after completing harvest chores. It's also known as the Wine Moon because grapes are now ready to be picked and fermented. In China, it's known as the Mid-Autumn Moon and marks a festival in honor of Chang-O, who is said to have saved starving people from a tyrannical king and become the moon. To celebrate, moon cakes are eaten in her honor while the celebrants watch the moon rise.

ALTERNATE NAMES Apple Moon, Chrysanthemum Moon, Mid-Autumn Moon, Singing Moon, Wine Moon

ANIMALS donkey, jackal, pig

COLORS brown, orange, yellow

CRYSTALS Citrine, Green Jadeite Jade, Orange Calcite

DEITIES Abundantia, Annona, Ch'ang-O, Hestia, Isis, Vesta

ESSENTIAL OILS anise, clary sage, copal

HERBS bay, fennel, witch hazel

KEYWORDS abundance, achievement, receiving

CITRINE Citrine is a stone of abundance and as such it pairs perfectly with the Harvest Moon. It's connected to the Roman goddess Abundantia, who's the keeper of the cornucopia. Citrine attracts an abundance of all things. Now's the time to make great leaps toward anything you've had in mind as a long-term goal.

GREEN JADEITE JADE Jade makes an excellent companion during the time of the Harvest Moon because of its association with health, wealth, and luck. The fruits of your labor will nourish your mind, body, and spirit. Jade keeps your energy reserves full by accumulating universal energy and storing it in your field for later use. It also helps good luck find its way to you.

ORANGE CALCITE This stone mimics the color that's so often visible in the Harvest Moon when it sits just above the horizon. Orange Calcite warms the body and the soul, preparing you to move into the cooler autumn months.

The Blood Moon

The Blood Moon is so named because it occurs during the time of the hunt. After the domestication of livestock, this moon became associated with the time that animals were slaughtered for food. This moon is also known as the Falling Leaf Moon because this is when trees drop their leaves.

ALTERNATE NAMES Falling Leaf Moon, Kindly Moon, Moon of the Changing Seasons, Sanguine Moon, Shedding Moon, Ten Colds Moon

ANIMALS bat, crow, scorpion

COLORS black, red, teal

CRYSTALS Bloodstone, Pink Tourmaline, Ruby

DEITIES Anubis, Durga, Herne, Kali, Lakshmi, Saraswati

ESSENTIAL OILS copal, sandalwood, spearmint

HERBS burdock, thyme, wormwood

KEYWORDS challenge, journey, triumph

BLOODSTONE This stone is dark green with patches of red that resemble spots of blood. It connects you with your primal self, allowing you to focus on your most basic needs. Although this may be viewed as selfish, it's fulfilling to focus on nourishing your physical body through eating and sleeping.

PINK TOURMALINE This crystal is one of the October birthstones, but it is also suited to the energy of the Blood Moon. Its color ranges from pink to magenta, and it has a strong, invigorating energy. Reach for this stone if you become lethargic or feel yourself longing for sunshine. Carrying it provides an exhilarating burst of energy as it channels the anticipation of the hunt.

RUBY Ruby is associated with the lifeblood that flows through all living things. It is used to bring energy into the physical body for healing. This stone has a special tie to Hindu goddesses such as Durga, Kali, Lakshmi, and Saraswati, but it has a particular affinity with Kali, the destroyer goddess of liberation and protection. One of the most well-known myths about Kali is her defeat of the demon Raktabija by drinking his blood. Although this may seem gruesome, it was actually an act of protection. Ruby is thought to embody this protective energy with its blood-red color.

To connect with the energy of the *Blood Moon*, collect some red leaves from outdoors and bring them into your sacred space as a reminder of the changing seasons. Take a few minutes to write down a list of self-care activities that nourish your physical body. Then, set a Bloodstone atop the leaves. Each time you see this crystal in your sacred space, perform one of the actions on your list.

To connect with the *Snow Moon*, place a white candle in your sacred space. Hold a Selenite or Clear Quartz crystal and connect to spirit. Set the stone near the candle, light the candle, and focus on the flame. Close your eyes and allow sensations, thoughts, and feelings to leave you. Bring your attention to what remains; this is where you connect with spirit.

NOVEMBER

The Snow Moon

The Snow Moon is so named because this is the time of year when
the first snow begins to fall. This is also how the Chinese name for
this moon, the White Moon, came into being.

ALTERNATE NAMES Crone Moon,
Morning Moon, Tree Moon, White Moon

ANIMALS swan, white fox, white tiger

COLORS gold, indigo, white

CRYSTALS Clear Quartz, Ethiopian Opal,
Selenite

DEITIES Khione, Kuraokami, Maman
Brigitte, Marzanna, Poli'ahu, Skadi

ESSENTIAL OILS blue cypress, camphor,
eucalyptus

HERBS clove, copaiba, turmeric

KEYWORDS detachment, illumination,
spirituality

CLEAR QUARTZ Clear Quartz helps create
mental clarity like no other stone. It lets you
step into another realm of consciousness so
that you're able to see through the illusion
of living in duality as a physical and spiritual
being. Work with this stone during the time of
the Snow Moon if you're ready to understand
the importance of detachment and integrate

this spiritual lesson into your daily life. Clear
Quartz reminds you that you are a spiritual
being having a human experience, and
although there are problems that can easily
flood our human ego-mind, these are often
trivial when viewed from the perspective of
your true, spiritual self.

ETHIOPIAN OPAL This gem displays
a brilliance that is truly radiant. Its rainbow
flashes of light are a metaphor for illumination
and our own spiritual awakening. Ethiopian
Opal helps you find the stillness in day-to-day
moments so that you can appreciate what you
have and be fully present for the experience.

SELENITE Selenite is a crystal of purity
and light. Its high frequency elevates your
consciousness to places where you can
see what's truly important in life. It brings
through an energy that's similar to the quiet
and stillness you'd find on a crisp, snowy day,
and it perfectly complements the energy of
the Snow Moon.

The Cold Moon

The Cold Moon is named for the time when the coldness of winter takes hold.
It's known as the Oak Moon by some modern Pagans because it's the time of
the Lord, whose symbol is the oak tree. The name Oak Moon is also
used to describe the strength of the oak tree because it's able to
withstand tough winters.

ALTERNATE NAMES Bitter Moon,
Christmas Moon, Darkest Moon, Feast Moon,
Moon Before Yule, Oak Moon

ANIMALS badger, falcon, goat

COLORS black, indigo, silver

CRYSTALS Dumortierite, Lapis Lazuli,
Shattuckite

DEITIES Amaterasu, Baldur, Hades, Hodr,
Thor, Zeus

ESSENTIAL OILS blue tansy, melissa,
silver fir

HERBS black cohosh, holly, mistletoe

KEYWORDS darkness, rest, shadow side

DUMORTIERITE This stone embodies the
Danish hygge lifestyle and encourages you to
get cozy. It's perfect to work with during the
time of the Cold Moon, when there's nothing
nicer than snuggling up by the fire with friends,
family, and a cup of hot cocoa. Dumortierite is
a stone of "warm fuzzies" and aids those who
feel blue when winter temperatures plummet.

LAPIS LAZULI Lapis Lazuli has been
known as a stone of spiritual mystery as far
back as ancient Egypt. This crystal helps you
understand your shadow side—the part of
you that you're unaware of or that you may
not want to acknowledge. This is the part of
yourself that encompasses the challenging
aspects of your personality. Although the
shadow self is often ignored, consciously
working with it brings about personal growth.
The time of the Cold Moon is best spent
retreating inward to create positive change.
Lapis helps you tap into your shadow side and
take a journey of self-discovery.

SHATTUCKITE This crystal facilitates
shamanic journey work. The Cold Moon is a
time to journey inward and sweep away the
darkness that has accumulated during the year.
It's the time to release negative emotions and
patterns.

On the night of the *Cold Moon*, gather a goblet, a container of water, and a Shattuckite stone. Identify any emotions or patterns you'd like to release and pour some water into the goblet. Once it's full, hold your Shattuckite and consider how the goblet represents you; it's a vessel filled with emotions and patterns. When you're ready, release them by tossing the water from the goblet onto the earth.

The Blue Moon

The term *Blue Moon* dates back to the sixteenth century, when instead of "when pigs fly" people would say "when the moon is blue." It later evolved to mean something that occurred only rarely and described a fourth full moon in a season (which occurs about once every nineteen years). Within the last hundred years, the term has evolved to mean the second full moon in a month.

ALTERNATE NAMES Spirit Moon

ANIMALS blue jay, heron, indigo bunting, moon jellyfish, peacock

COLORS blue, light blue, indigo

CRYSTALS Blue Lace Agate, Blue Quartz, Rainbow Moonstone

DEITIES Aksobhya, Amun, Hapi, Melek Ta'us, Shiva, Vishnu

ESSENTIAL OILS blue tansy, helichrysum, sage

HERBS borage, santolina, speedwell

KEYWORDS spontaneity, surprises, wonder

BLUE LACE AGATE This is a stone of hope, but it also promotes spontaneity. Rather than going through the motions to achieve your goals and reach your dreams, allow Spirit to guide you toward what you want from life. Blue Lace Agate reminds you that you just need to follow the path that Spirit has placed before you, even if you're still unsure where it leads. This crystal gives you courage to try new things and have new experiences, even when they challenge you.

BLUE QUARTZ This stone is excellent for focus and for living in the present moment. It creates a feeling of clarity and an appreciation for the surprises that life may bring your way.

RAINBOW MOONSTONE Rainbow Moonstone evokes the mystery and sense of wonder of the Blue Moon. This crystal enhances your intuition and helps you see more than what lies at the surface. This stone instills a desire to explore the hidden realms and promotes spiritual curiosity. Work with Rainbow Moonstone when you want to peel back the layers of a situation to reveal the spiritual lessons being shared with you.

During the *Blue Moon*, light a blue candle in your sacred space and set it and a Blue Lace Agate stone in front of you. Turn off all other lights in the space. Looking at the Blue Lace Agate, let your gaze soften. Close your eyes and think about a great journey, physical or spiritual, that you'd like to take. Ask the universe to lead you on it. Allow yourself to be immersed in the experience. When you feel ready, open your eyes and extinguish the candle.

CHAPTER 6

Crystals for the 13 Native Moons

The thirteen Native Moons described in this section were collected from the rich and varied stories and cultural traditions of many different Native American tribes. Finding common threads among the wisdom of these tribes is not always easy, however, there is some overlap in these moon names and their associations. The names given here are some of the most commonly used among the Algonquin tribes, while the alternative names come from other well-known tribal peoples from the Americas.

January: The Old Moon	130
February: The Frost Moon	132
March: The Crow Moon	135
April: The Fish Moon	137
May: The Flower Moon	139
June: The Strawberry Moon	140
July: The Buck Moon	143
August: The Grain Moon	144
September: The Fruit Moon	146
October: The Hunter's Moon	149
November: The Beaver Moon	151
December: The Long Nights Moon	152
Blue: The Azure Moon	155

The Old Moon

The Old Moon is so named for its Cree name, "The Moon When the Old Fellow Spreads the Brush." It also signifies the peak of winter weather before we begin to move toward spring warmth and growth.

ALTERNATE NAMES Bear Hunting Moon, Goose Moon, Great Spirit Moon, Moon of Life at Its Height, Moon of the Cedar Dust Wind, Moon When the Old Fellow Spreads the Brush

ANIMALS bear, goose, wolf

COLORS blue, peach, white

CRYSTALS Blue Chalcedony, Peach Moonstone, Snowflake Obsidian

DEITIES Aincekoko, Chibiabos, Mashkuapeu the Bear Master, Muwin, Nisk-Napeu the Goose Master, Viracocha

ESSENTIAL OILS cedar, rose, vanilla

HERBS marshmallow, mullein, peppermint

KEYWORDS ancestors, traditions, wisdom

BLUE CHALCEDONY Blue Chalcedony has a very gentle energy. It is almost ethereal and enhances your connection with those on the other side who have important messages to share with you. A high-energy stone, this crystal only allows contact with those spirits or ancestors who are working for your highest good. It protects you from any negative entities.

PEACH MOONSTONE This soft, feminine-energy stone embodies ancient wisdom and guidance. Its shimmering surface encourages inner reflection and awakens your memories of friends and family. The support of loved ones becomes especially important during this harsh time of year, and group cooperation and unity should take precedence over individual desires. Peach Moonstone reminds you of this and of the important lessons passed down to you from the older and wiser members of your family and community.

SNOWFLAKE OBSIDIAN The time of the Old Moon is a time for reflection and rest. It is perfect for honoring ancestor spirits. Obsidian of all kinds has been used for ancestor work and shamanic journeying by both ancient and modern peoples. Snowflake Obsidian encourages ancestral connection and creates a touch point for remembrance and the honoring of your ancestors.

To connect with the energy of the *Old Moon*, anoint a black candle with cedar oil by rubbing a drop or two over its surface. Light the candle, and place it near a Snowflake Obsidian stone and a picture of your ancestors. Ask for any wisdom or knowledge that they'd like to impart, and look for signs, symbols, or messages that come through over the next few days.

The Frost Moon

The Frost Moon is named for the frost that occurs at this time. It has also been known as the Hunger Moon or the Starvation Moon by some tribes, because game would become scarce by February, making for a difficult hunt, resulting in hungry bellies. Stored food would also start to run out this time of year, meaning there was less to eat all around.

ALTERNATE NAMES Bony Moon, Hunger Moon, Little Famine Moon, Raccoon Moon, Seal Pup Moon, Starvation Moon

ANIMALS bobcat, racoon, seal

COLORS rainbow (all colors)

CRYSTALS Chrysanthemum Stone, Diamond, Pink Aventurine

DEITIES Azeban, Mishipesha, Sedna, Toho Kachina, Tokoch Kachina, Viracocha

ESSENTIAL OILS spearmint, spruce

HERBS fir, sage, yarrow

KEYWORDS cunning, radiance, reflection

CHRYSANTHEMUM STONE This rock is formed when a whitish mineral, commonly Celestine, creates a flower-shaped growth on shale or one of several other dark, metamorphic stones. It can be used to connect with the energy of the Frost Moon. This stone holds an inner radiance that's just waiting to blossom.

Chrysanthemum Stone helps you discover your own inner light. It teaches you how to be more independent and reclaim your power if you have given it away to another.

DIAMOND No crystal on Earth is as brilliant as the Diamond. It helps you reflect on your past, present, and future, so you understand lessons and embrace the wisdom that is to be gained from your experiences. This information gives you insight into the best path forward so that you can use cunning and skill for your highest good.

PINK AVENTURINE This gentle stone radiates with an inner fire of peace and compassion. It inspires you to reflect on your own situation and life circumstances so that you can better relate to others. It's a stone for empaths, allowing you to make heartfelt connections while keeping healthy energetic boundaries.

To connect with the energy of the **Frost Moon**, trace the outline of your hand on a piece of paper and draw a spiral on the palm. This represents the power you have as a spiritual being. You may fill the rest of the paper with symbols, affirmations, or anything else that fills you up with positive energy. Place this drawing in your sacred space, and set a Chrysanthemum Stone over the palm. This is a reminder to set boundaries and hold onto your power rather than allow yourself to give it away to others.

To connect with the energy of the *Crow Moon*, place a small scrap of black cloth in a dish to form a makeshift nest. Put one Black Tourmaline, Blue Apatite, or Rainbow Fluorite stone (or one of each) in the nest. Ask that the crow shares his medicine with you to provide a new perspective on your current situation.

The Crow Moon

The Crow Moon is named for the period when crows return at the end of their migration. Their cawing is a sign of the end of winter. Some tribes know it as the Worm Moon because when the ground thaws, earthworms become active, and hungry birds return to the land. Other tribes have known the March full moon as the Crust Moon, for the crust formed on snow by repeated freezing and thawing. Still others called this moon the Sap Moon or Sugar Moon because it's when maple trees are tapped. Another name is the Sore Eye Moon, named for the glare created by sunlight reflecting off the snow.

ALTERNATE NAMES Crust Moon, Moon When Eyes Are Sore from the Bright Snow, Sap Moon, Sore Eye Moon, Sugar Moon, Worm Moon

ANIMALS butterfly, crow, robin

COLORS black, light blue, violet

CRYSTALS Black Tourmaline, Blue Apatite, Rainbow Fluorite

DEITIES Butterfly Maiden, Crow Mother, Opeechee, Palhik Mana

ESSENTIAL OILS blue tansy, clary sage, copal

HERBS dandelion, skullcap, wormwood

KEYWORDS cunning, intelligence, wit

BLACK TOURMALINE The shiny, black surface of this stone mimics the intensity of crow feathers. Black Tourmaline is a grounding crystal, connecting you with earth energy. It ties you to the physical world and centers you in the present moment. Black Tourmaline reawakens your wit and instinct to provide wisdom and guidance where it's needed most.

BLUE APATITE Blue Apatite stimulates the mental body, making this the perfect crystal to connect with the cunning crow totem. Work with this stone when change is on the horizon and you need to call upon your intellect and wit to help you navigate the path ahead.

RAINBOW FLUORITE This crystal is known for providing mental clarity. It pairs with Black Tourmaline and Blue Apatite to shed some light on your current situation. It's also excellent for transforming negative vibrations into positive energy.

To connect with the energy of the *Fish Moon*, make a list of three new things you'd like to do. Tie a pink ribbon around a Rhodochrosite stone as a symbol of the commitment you've made to begin this new journey and set it near the list in your sacred space. When you've completed your list, untie the ribbon and hang it as a reminder of your accomplishment.

APRIL
The Fish Moon

The Fish Moon is named for the spawning time when shad, members of the herring family, swim upstream. It has also been known by some tribes as the Pink Moon because one of the earliest flowers, wild ground phlox— also known as moss pinks or grass pinks—begin to bloom.

ALTERNATE NAMES Egg Moon, Frog Moon, Moon When Geese Return in Scattered Formation, Pink Moon, Snow Melt Moon, Sprouting Grass Moon

ANIMALS fish, frog, goose

COLORS light blue, light green, pink

CRYSTALS Larimar, Rhodochrosite, Tugtupite

DEITIES Akwulabemu, Anika-Peu the Frog Master, Huitzilopochtli, Lucifee, Paakwa Kachina, Tokoch Kachina

ESSENTIAL OILS carnation, rose, sweetgrass

HERBS beargrass, sweetgrass, wild licorice

KEYWORDS fertility, growth, harmony

LARIMAR Larimar has deep connection to all the waters of the world and an affinity with dolphins and fish. This stone embodies a "go with the flow" energy and helps you release attachment to doing things in a particular way. Larimar is here to support you in achieving your goals and dreams, but rather than letting you fight the current to get there, it shows you how to relax and be in flow. Larimar shows you that you will still reach your desired result, but the journey can be much easier than you're making it.

RHODOCHROSITE Rhodochrosite has long been used as a symbol of fertility, as it resembles the tissue of the womb. This crystal is a perfect companion to harness the energy of the spawning shad during the time of the Fish Moon. However, it can also be symbolic of a great journey resulting in personal growth.

TUGTUPITE This newly discovered, rare stone from Greenland is the ultimate harmony stone. Its intense pink color is rarely found in natural crystals, but it instantly awakens the Heart Chakra and encourages self-love and inner balance. Tugtupite brings in waves of bliss and feelings of oneness.

To connect with the energy of the *Flower Moon*, bring a vase of fresh flowers into your space. Place a Rainforest Jasper stone into the vase to facilitate a connection to the energy of the blossoms. Make time to sit with the flowers daily and show your gratitude for the happiness and abundance that nature makes available to you.

The Flower Moon

The Flower Moon is named for the time of year when flowers bloom in abundance. Some tribes have a legend that flowers dance in the moonlight in honor of this moon on the night of the Flower Moon. Other tribes know this as the Corn Planting Moon because this is the time of year when corn seed is ready to be sown.

ALTERNATE NAMES Budding Moon, Corn Planting Moon, Grass Moon, Milk Moon, Panther Moon, Planting Moon

ANIMALS cow, panther, snake

COLORS green, orange, yellow

CRYSTALS Heliodor, Peridot, Rainforest Jasper

DEITIES Coatlicue, Pitaskog, Quetzalcoatl, Situlili, Snake-Woman, Unktehi

ESSENTIAL OILS lavender, neroli, ravensara

HERBS apple mint, catnip, peppermint

KEYWORDS bliss, happiness, joy

HELIODOR This yellow variety of Beryl looks as if it contains rays of the Sun itself. While honoring the Flower Moon is important, flowers couldn't grow without sunlight. Heliodor helps you shine your own light and encourages your gifts to blossom into being. This inspirational crystal supports you as you walk your soul path.

PERIDOT This bright green crystal vibrates with the frequency of growth and healing. It helps restore balance to your body, mind, and spirit so that you can live in a place of happiness and harmony. Peridot helps you sort out what is most important to you so that you can find bliss and joy wherever you look.

RAINFOREST JASPER This stone is deeply connected to nature and to Mother Earth herself. It encourages you to tune into the world around you. Work with this crystal when you're in need of soul-level healing and emotional restoration. By connecting to the natural rhythms of the Earth, you'll find more bliss and happiness through your relationship with the world around you.

The Strawberry Moon

The Strawberry Moon is named for the time of year when
strawberries ripen and are ready to harvest.

ALTERNATE NAMES Full Leaf Moon,
Green Corn Moon, Hot Moon, Hunting Moon

ANIMALS buffalo, ladybug, woodpecker

COLORS pink, red, yellow

CRYSTALS Amber, Mookaite Jasper,
Strawberry Quartz

DEITIES Camazotz, Evaki, Mosairu Kachina,
Papa'xes, Tamatz Kayaumari, White Buffalo
Calf Woman

ESSENTIAL OILS camphor, carrot seed,
sweetgrass

HERBS beargrass, desert sage, sweetgrass

KEYWORDS generosity, gratitude,
manifestation

AMBER Amber promotes manifesting
abundance and being generous with what you
have received. This crystal promotes sharing of
material goods, wisdom, love, and time. Amber
is known for enhancing attitudes of gratitude
and for bestowing a bounty of blessings upon
those who work with it. It's the perfect crystal
to work with during the time of the Strawberry
Moon, when all sweet things are in abundance.

MOOKAITE JASPER Mookaite Jasper
is a colorful stone with swirling tones of red,
white, yellow, and purple. It's best known for
its ability to enhance creative expression, but it
can also be used to co-create with the universe
for manifesting. Work with this stone when
you're ready to call in new energy and release
that which is no longer serving you. The key to
success with Mookaite is to be wholeheartedly
ready to receive.

STRAWBERRY QUARTZ This variety
of Quartz is named for the vibrant pink
strawberry fruit. True Strawberry Quartz
contains small, pink Rutile crystals in a matrix
of clear Quartz, but there are many other
commercially available crystals with this name.
Real Strawberry Quartz can be a little more
challenging to find—it is not the same as the
Pink Aventurine or man-made Cherry Quartz
that often share its name. Strawberry Quartz
helps bring out the sweetness in life, and it
encourages you to recognize and be grateful for
what you do have rather than focusing on what
you don't.

To connect with the energy of the *Strawberry Moon*, write a list of things you're ready to receive. On the evening of the Strawberry Moon, place the list on your altar and surround it with Mookaite Jasper (if you only have one stone, place it atop the list). Leave the list and stones in place until the next full moon.

To connect with the energy of the *Buck Moon*, place a Red Pyrope Garnet crystal atop an image of a buck. Hover your hands above the stone, and ask the buck to share his protective energy with you. When you feel you've made a connection with the energy, fold the picture around the stone and place it in your medicine pouch or mojo bag.

The Buck Moon

The Buck Moon is named for the time when male deer grow their velvet antlers. It has also been known by some tribes as the Thunder Moon because of the frequent thunderstorms this time of year.

ALTERNATE NAMES Crane Moon, Deer Moon, Dry Moon, Green Bean Moon, Ripe Corn Moon, Thunder Moon

ANIMALS buck, crane, deer

COLORS brown, green, orange

CRYSTALS Biggs Picture Jasper, Iolite, Red Pyrope Garnet

DEITIES Awi Usdi, Deer Woman, Khenkho, Sowi-Ingwu, Tamatz Kayaumari

ESSENTIAL OILS cypress, petitgrain, vetiver

HERBS basil, calendula, white angelica

KEYWORDS leadership, protection, spirit

BIGGS PICTURE JASPER This beautiful Jasper variety is not widely commercially available as it comes only from Oregon, USA. The swirling patterns on the surface of this stone look like petroglyphs and have a very ancient feel. Biggs Picture Jasper keeps you grounded while urging you to connect to Spirit in a deeper way. This is an excellent crystal for shamanic journey work and astral travel.

IOLITE Iolite was said to be used by the Vikings to aid in navigation as they sailed across the Atlantic. It's a stone of guidance today as well, and it partners particularly well with those who are natural leaders. Work with this stone when you find yourself in a position of authority, or when your passion for something urges you to take charge of a group. Iolite helps you balance the position of leader by encouraging you to make all in the group feel appreciated and respected while still moving forward toward your goal.

RED PYROPE GARNET This variety of Garnet embodies the strength and life force of the buck. It's a stone of vitality and power, but it is also highly protective. Just as a buck's antlers can be used for defense, the Red Pyrope Garnet can defend you against unwanted energies.

The Grain Moon

The Grain Moon is named for grains, such as corn and barley, that can now be harvested. Fishing tribes know this as the Sturgeon Moon, named after the fish that are abundant at this time. Other tribes know the August full moon as the Red Moon because it often takes on a reddish color. Still others call this the Lightning Moon due to frequent late-summer thunderstorms.

ALTERNATE NAMES Barley Moon, Lightning Moon, Red Moon, Sturgeon Moon, Swan Flight Moon, Women's Moon

ANIMALS squirrel, sturgeon, swan

COLORS gold, green, yellow

CRYSTALS Green Grossular Garnet, Heliodor, Ruby Fuchsite

DEITIES Laqan Kachina, Mashe-Namak, Mikew, Nisk-Napeu the Goose Master, Urubutsin

ESSENTIAL OILS rosewood, tangerine, tea tree

HERBS eucalyptus, lemongrass, rose petal

KEYWORDS abundance, connection, magic

GREEN GROSSULAR GARNET This abundance stone connects to the Grain Moon by reminding you that with hard work, there will be plenty to harvest down the road. Green Grossular Garnet enhances your connection to the plants and animals of the Earth. Work with this stone if you'd like to find balance between modern life and more traditional ways of living.

HELIODOR A yellow variety of Beryl, Heliodor shines with the color of golden grain. This crystal helps you recognize abundance all around you and connects you to all that is. The more connected and grateful you feel, the more you have to be thankful for, because things are drawn to you like a magnet. Helidor is also a stone of magic and facilitates mystical experiences.

RUBY FUCHSITE This rock, also called Anyolite, is a combination of two minerals, Ruby Fuchsite and Green Fuchsite. This crystal corresponds to the heart center and instills empathy and compassion. Wear Ruby Fuchsite in a medicine bag over your heart to facilitate a connection with others. This energy is perfectly suited to the Grain Moon, a time of celebration and sharing the abundant harvest.

To connect with the energy of the *Grain Moon*, place a small bowl of dry grains (e.g., corn, barley, or rice) in your sacred space or on your altar. Surround the bowl with Ruby Fuchsite stones to represent the sharing of this abundance with those you love. You may even choose to have one stone to represent each specific person in your circle of close friends and family.

SEPTEMBER
The Fruit Moon

The Fruit Moon is named for the time when tree fruits, such as apples, are ready to harvest.

ALTERNATE NAMES Leaves Turning Moon, Moon When the Deer Paw the Earth, Mulberry Moon, Nut Moon, Spider Web on the Ground at Dawn Moon, Yellow Leaf Moon

ANIMALS deer, spider, whale

COLORS burgundy, light blue, tan

CRYSTALS Pyrite, Red Calcite, Variscite

DEITIES Aumanil, Bootup, Inktomi, Moshup, Spider Grandmother, Vihio

ESSENTIAL OILS helichrysum, myrrh, vetiver

HERBS balsam fir, coriander, sweet marjoram

KEYWORDS joy, peace, pleasure

PYRITE This mineral stimulates happiness and joy. A strong and masculine stone, Pyrite invigorates the Solar Plexus Chakra and instills a sense of peace and contentment. It also encourages you to nourish yourself and take time for activities that bring you pleasure, such as painting, making music, or cooking a good meal.

RED CALCITE Red Calcite is one of the less common colors of Calcite, but it's extremely powerful. The red color taps into your Root Chakra, your earthly pleasure center, and stimulates sexual and creative energies. This crystal helps you dive into your primal creativity and encourages you to express yourself as a spiritual being here on Earth.

VARISCITE This unusual stone is a seafoam green mineral in a tan matrix. It has a peaceful, tranquil energy that is excellent for meditation. It pairs well with the energy of the Fruit Moon because it helps you reflect upon the sweet things in life. This appreciation and inner reflection can be very personal and specific to you, or it can be about things that are appreciated by all (e.g., beautiful sunsets, a cool breeze on a warm day, or the sound of crickets chirping at night). Variscite helps you pause and be truly present in the beauty that surrounds you so you can let the joy of the moment fill your heart.

To connect with the energy of the *Fruit Moon*, hold a Pyrite, Red Calcite, or Variscite crystal in your hands and hover them above a piece of tree fruit. Send energy to the fruit. Set down your crystal and pick up the fruit. Close your eyes and bite the fruit. Allow yourself to be immersed in the pleasure of eating it.

During the *Hunter's Moon*, create a medicine bag by filling a small pouch with dried lavender and Celestite, Red Jasper, and/or Stromatolite. You may also choose to include other things such as feathers, charms, shells, or any other objects that are sacred to you. Charge and empower your medicine bag by placing it on your altar on the evening of the Hunter's Moon. This is now an amulet for personal strength or protection. You may wear it or keep it on your altar.

The Hunter's Moon

The Hunter's Moon is named for the time when the leaves have fallen from the trees and the fields are clear of crops, so fattened game is easy to spot. The evening of the Hunter's Moon is a special feast day to celebrate the bounty of food that was available. Some tribes have known this as the Travel Moon because hunters needed to follow migratory game during this time. It's also sometimes called the Moon When the Gopher Looks Back, in reference to the gopher longingly looking backward toward the long-gone summer months.

ALTERNATE NAMES Blackberry Moon, Dying Moon, Moon When Quilling and Beading Are Done, Moon When the Gopher Looks Back, Raven Moon, Travel Moon

ANIMALS gopher, porcupine, raven

COLORS brown, red, teal

CRYSTALS Celestite, Red Jasper, Stromatolite

DEITIES Mixcoatl, Old Woman Gopher, Opochtli, Porcupine Master, Qanglaagix, Tulukaruq

ESSENTIAL OILS cedar, fennel, sweet marjoram

HERBS lavender, lemongrass, peppermint

KEYWORDS dignity, honor, respect

CELESTITE Celestite acts like a gateway to the spirit world. It invites and welcomes your guardians into your space. Work with this crystal if you'd like to call upon your ancestors or spirit guides for guidance and support. Celestite helps you honor these beings by creating sacred space in which to connect with them.

RED JASPER Red Jasper is a stone of reverence and dignity, and it mimics the honor and respect that was shown to animals that were killed during the hunt. This stone has a primal energy, and it allows you to better understand the Earth's natural cycles and the cycles of life and death.

STROMATOLITE Stromatolite is a stone formed by layers of fossilized algae. It instills a sense of respect for the Earth, helping you understand that the very ground you walk upon is made of the remains of the plants and animals that lived before you. This is a stone of reverence and helps you appreciate the sacredness of all things.

To connect with the energy of the *Beaver Moon*, place some dried allspice berries and a Rainbow Sheen Obsidian stone in a small pouch. Tuck it into your pillowcase. Before you go to sleep, set the intention to experience and remember a meaningful dream that will provide you with guidance about something that needs to be healed in your life.

The Beaver Moon

The Beaver Moon is named for the time of year when traps were set to collect furs for winter clothing. Other tribes have known this moon as the Fog Moon, Frosty Moon, and the Moon of Storms because the weather was rapidly shifting from the end of autumn to the bitter cold of winter.

ALTERNATE NAMES Fog Moon, Frosty Moon, Moon of Storms, Moon When Deer Shed Antlers, Sassafras Moon, Trading Moon

ANIMALS beaver, deer, scorpion

COLORS brown, gray, green, indigo

CRYSTALS Petrified Wood, Rainbow Sheen Obsidian, Shungite

DEITIES Aisoyimstan, Itztlacoliuhqui, Khuno, Negafook

ESSENTIAL OILS camphor, lemon verbena, vanilla

HERBS allspice, cinquefoil, wood betony

KEYWORDS courage, ingenuity, persistence

PETRIFIED WOOD Petrified Wood has a special connection to the beaver totem. It represents the persistence needed to overcome the obstacles blocking your path. This stone helps you accomplish anything you set your mind to by taking things one step at a time.

Work with Petrified Wood when you must undertake a daunting task to help keep you motivated and on track throughout the process.

RAINBOW SHEEN OBSIDIAN This crystal is revered for its ability to enhance shamanic journey and astral travel. It promotes intense dreamwork and is an excellent companion stone for any mystical experience. Journeying within the self or to other realms takes a great deal of courage. Rainbow Sheen Obsidian supports you while you take these discoveries head-on and bring back powerful lessons that can be applied to your everyday life.

SHUNGITE This stone is well known for claims about its ability to purify energy. This ancient crystal carries the energy of ingenuity. The full list of Shungite's uses is not yet known to us, but this stone seems to constantly be encouraging us to learn more, to do more, and to push onward toward the next breakthrough.

The Long Nights Moon

The Long Nights Moon is named for when the days grow shorter and the nights lengthen. Some tribes knew this as the Moon of Popping Trees, because it gets so cold that you can hear branches freezing and snapping. It has also been known as the Deer Shed Their Horns Moon in recognition of the time when deer begin to drop their annual antlers.

ALTERNATE NAMES Big Winter Moon, Dark Night Moon, Deer Shed Their Horns Moon, Little Spirit Moon, Moon of Popping Trees, Peach Moon

ANIMALS deer, mouse, snowy owl

COLORS black, light blue, silver

CRYSTALS Aquamarine, Hessonite Garnet, Peach Selenite

DEITIES Awi Usdi, Big Owl, Mouse Woman, Sowi-Ingwu, Uhua-Peu the Owl Master, Warrior Mouse

ESSENTIAL OILS balsam fir, pine, wintergreen

HERBS bayberry, chamomile, mistletoe

KEYWORDS introspection, patience, stillness

AQUAMARINE This blue variety of Beryl perfectly captures the peace and stillness of this time of year. It's a stone of calm and tranquility, and it helps you focus on the here and now. The long, dark nights create space for the expansion of your conscious mind. Aquamarine helps you tune into your thoughts and bring them from your subconscious into present moment awareness. This stone helps you relax into silence rather than fighting it by filling it with mental chatter.

HESSONITE GARNET This dark time of year is associated with feminine energy, or yin. This energy is receptive, nurturing, and gentle. Hessonite embodies these divine feminine qualities in a way that promotes empathy, compassion, self-love, and deep healing. Work with Hessonite if you feel called to restore your mind, body, and spirit through acts of self-care.

PEACH SELENITE This crystal ranges in color from soft peach to vibrant apricot. It's connected to the Sacral Chakra and promotes gentle healing through self-expression. Peach Selenite holds space for you to tap into your creative fire.

To connect with the energy of the *Long Nights Moon*, light an orange candle for creativity and a blue candle for self-expression. Place them in your sacred space. Gather some watercolor paints, paintbrushes, paper, a jar of water, and an Aquamarine crystal. Place the Aquamarine in the jar of water and use it to create a crystal energy–infused watercolor painting.

To connect with the energy of the *Azure Moon*, hold a Sunstone in your hands or place it in front of you. Think about the gifts you have to share with the world that you may be holding back. Make a list of these contributions and call upon your Sunstone each time you need strength or support to shine your light.

BLUE

The Azure Moon

The Azure Moon is an alternative name for the Blue Moon.

ALTERNATE NAMES Blue Moon

ANIMALS blue dart frog, butterfly

COLORS blue, indigo, light blue

CRYSTALS Blue Kyanite, Pink Spinel, Sunstone

DEITIES Akwulabemu, Anika-Peu the Frog Master, Chaac, Paakwa Kachina, Palhik Mana, Tlaloc

ESSENTIAL OILS blue spruce, sage, sweetgrass

HERBS agave, blue spruce, yarrow

KEYWORDS belonging, intimacy, second chances

BLUE KYANITE This royal blue stone has a high vibrational energy and is a powerful cleanser. This makes it a great companion for the Azure Moon, the moon of second chances. If you've missed an opportunity or made a miscalculation, this is the time to revisit the situation and ask the universe for a do-over. Whatever was an obstacle in the past was there to help you learn an important lesson, but now you can move forward with wisdom and support.

PINK SPINEL This crystal brings balance to the intensity of the Azure Moon. It creates more intimacy in your life, whether with friends, romantic partners, family members, or new acquaintances. Pink Spinel helps you push your limits (in a good way!) when it comes to closeness and trust, and it encourages you to embrace the unknown. This crystal helps you take a leap of faith in your relationships so that you're able to experience the sweet rewards that closeness with others brings into your life.

SUNSTONE We all live under one sun. This sense of belonging is at the core of Sunstone's energetic vibration. A constant reminder of oneness and of the interconnectedness of all creatures, this crystal helps you discover what it's like to truly feel that you belong. Sunstone is helpful for introverts, as it embodies joy and reminds you that all beings have value. Everyone has something to contribute to this world, so release fear or blocks and shine your light!

CHAPTER 7

Crystals for the 13 Celtic Moons

The thirteen Celtic Moons described in this section are common to many modern practitioners of Celtic magic, including neo-Druidism. While the ancient Druids were known for their magic and healing abilities, most of their wisdom was lost throughout the ages, and although not much is known about the Druids, they still play an important role in modern Celtic spirituality. These modern practitioners associate the moon months names with the Neo-Pagan Celtic tree calendar, which is said to be derived from the Ogham alphabet system, although the authenticity of this association is hotly contested among scholars. The Ogham, or Celtic tree alphabet, was used to write an early form of the Irish language.

January: The Birch Moon	159
February: The Rowan Moon	160
March: The Ash Moon	163
April: The Alder Moon	164
May: The Willow Moon	166
June: The Hawthorn Moon	169
July: The Oak Moon	170
August: The Holly Moon	173
September: The Hazel Moon	175
October: The Vine Moon	176
November: The Reed Moon	178
December: The Elder Moon	181
Blue: The Ivy Moon	183

To connect with the energy of the *Birch Moon*, gather some birch twigs, tie them into a bundle, and hang them over your front door. If you're feeling creative, draw or paint the twigs and hang their image near the door. Place a Howlite stone nearby to welcome the positive, abundant energy of the Birch Moon into your home.

The Birch Moon

The Birch Moon is so named for the birch tree from the month of January in the Celtic Ogham tree calendar. It's connected to fertility, birth and rebirth, and the coming together of energies to create something new.

ALTERNATE NAMES Anabantids Moon, Beith Moon, Cold-Time Moon, Moon of Beginning, Moon of Inception, Quiet Moon

ANIMALS egret, pheasant, white stag

COLORS green, tan, white

CRYSTALS Connemara Marble, Emerald, Howlite

DEITIES Blodewedd, Ceridwen, Damara, Epona, Flidais the Lady of the Woods, the Morrigan

ESSENTIAL OILS clary sage, fennel, ylang

HERBS anise, birch, yarrow

KEYWORDS creativity, fertility, union

CONNEMARA MARBLE This green Serpentine from Ireland is known for its swirling patterns. It is a stone of abundance, and it makes a perfect companion for the energy of the Birch Moon. It has a natural connection to the energy of nature and to both birth—literal and figurative—and rebirth (of ideas, projects, etc.).

EMERALD Emerald has long been associated with fertility, as has the Birch Moon. This green variety of Beryl has a powerful energy and calls forth the divine feminine presence of Mother Earth through Flidais, the Lady of the Woods. Work with this stone during the time of the Birch Moon to create an abundance of all things in your life. Be careful to keep your thoughts positive so that you only call forth that which is for your highest good.

HOWLITE Howlite's white body with gray streaks looks like the white bark of the birch tree. When there is bare land, the birch is one of the first to grow to create a forest. Similarly, Howlite encourages new ideas to sprout forth from a blank mind. Clear your mind and meditate with this stone for guidance about how to start fresh or create a positive new beginning when something important in your life is coming to an end.

The Rowan Moon

The Rowan Moon is so named because it corresponds to the rowan tree, also known as the Mountain Ash, from the month of February in the Celtic Ogham tree calendar. It is connected to the hearth and home, the fire element, family and motherhood, divination and intuition, healing, astral travel, power and success, and protection.

ALTERNATE NAMES Astral Travel Moon, Luis Moon, Moon of Ice, Moon of Vision, Spirit Moon, Stay Home Time Moon

ANIMALS crane, duck, quail

COLORS black, gray, green

CRYSTALS Aragonite, Red Spinel, Vanadinite

DEITIES Beira, Boann, Branwen, Brighid/Brigit/Brigantia, Cailleach Bheur

ESSENTIAL OILS basil, bergamot, helichrysum

HERBS lemongrass, peppermint, willow

KEYWORDS community, family, kinship

ARAGONITE This crystal can appear in many colors and formations, but the best for connecting with the energy of the Rowan Moon is the sputnik variety. Sputnik Aragonite stones are rounded clusters of individual barrel-shaped crystals. These groupings are the perfect metaphor for harmony in your family or community. This crystal is lovely for group cooperation and helping to get everyone on the same page. Aragonite helps strengthen your relationships, bringing you closer to those you love. It's also a great stone to help you connect with others over a common cause.

RED SPINEL This deep red crystal taps into the fiery energy of the rowan. This tree produces vibrant red-orange berries that last all winter and create little pops of color in an otherwise dull winter landscape. Red Spinel is similar in that it adds excitement to your everyday routine. This crystal helps you really appreciate even the small moments in life and the interactions you have with others.

VANADINITE This vibrant mineral often appears sprinkled atop Barite clusters or in large groupings of plate-like crystals grouped together in a showy arrangement. The cheery energy of this stone enhances feelings of kinship and strengthens bonds between family members.

To connect with the energy of the *Rowan Moon*, write the names of your family members in a circle on a piece of paper. Place an Aragonite sputnik in the center of the circle to enhance kinship and family bonds. If there's a particular family member you'd like to connect with during this full moon, add a small Quartz crystal pointing from the Aragonite toward their name.

To connect with the energy of the *Ash Moon*, draw a small sketch of a tree and set a Green Aventurine stone (or several) on it to create a gemstone leaf canopy. Sit near your crystal tree each morning for a mini meditation, and ponder the ways you can continue to "branch out" in your life.

The Ash Moon

The Ash Moon is so named because it corresponds to the ash tree from the month of March in the Celtic Ogham tree calendar. It is connected to magic, the inner self, the water element, karma, imagination, love, focus, prosperity, intuition, and dreams. It was also known as the Chaste Moon because of its association with the purity of fresh soil ready to be seeded with spring crops.

ALTERNATE NAMES Chaste Moon, Cutios Moon, Nion Moon, Seeds Moon, Tree of Life Moon, Winds Moon

ANIMALS moth, seal, turtle

COLORS green, light blue, white

CRYSTALS Green Aventurine, Morganite, Pink Stilbite

DEITIES the Green Man, Gwydion, the Morrighan, Verbeia, Vivien the Lady of the Lake

ESSENTIAL OILS lavender, lotus, pine

HERBS patchouli, solomon's seal, sweet woodruff

KEYWORDS expansion, growth, success

GREEN AVENTURINE This crystal embodies growth and the act of branching out toward new experiences and ways of being. Commonly used for balancing the Heart Chakra, this crystal encourages deep, personal transformation and helps you find true success in your life by nudging you toward your soul path.

MORGANITE Morganite is a pink variety of Beryl that radiates with compassion. It supports gratitude and generosity, and it encourages the positivity that you send out into the universe to return to you tenfold. It's also a great companion crystal for inviting more love into your life—whether from yourself or from others.

PINK STILBITE This member of the Zeolite mineral group commonly forms pink, bowtie-shaped crystals. Pink Stilbite encourages you to explore new horizons, both inner and outer, so that you're able to expand your way of thinking and your sphere of consciousness. Work with it when you're embarking on new adventures or just stepping a little outside of your comfort zone. Stilbite's loving energy will help you feel supported, while gently pushing you further.

The Alder Moon

The Alder Moon is named for its correspondence to the alder tree from the
month of April in the Celtic Ogham tree calendar. It's connected
to the elements of water and air, balance, divination,
protection, passion, and confidence.

ALTERNATE NAMES Fearn Moon,
Giamonios Moon, Moon of Efficacy, Moon
of Self-Guidance, Moon of Utility, Shoots
Show Moon

ANIMALS bear, dog, seagull

COLORS blue, purple, red

CRYSTALS Auralite-23, Azurite,
Kambaba Jasper

DEITIES Babd Catha, Bran, Habetrot,
Lugh, Macha, Neit

ESSENTIAL OILS benzoin, black
pepper, neroli

HERBS bergamot, blue spruce,
jasmine flower

KEYWORDS intuition, prophecy, spirituality

AURALITE-23 This crystal is a special
variety of Amethyst from Ontario, Canada. It
instantly jump-starts your intuition. If you're
interested in developing your psychic skills,
learning to astral travel, or gaining insight
from your dreams, this stone is perfect for
you. It pairs especially well with the Alder
Moon because this moon promotes intuitive
development and teaches you to trust your
inner compass.

AZURITE This indigo crystal is well known
for enhancing your intuition and stimulating
your Third Eye Chakra. Place a piece over your
brow to connect with the universe in a deeper
way and call forth the messages it's trying to
share with you. The copper in this stone acts
like a conduit for energy, channeling it straight
into your pineal gland, your body's receiver for
cosmic wisdom. Hold Azurite in your hands
to help you interpret the messages, words, or
symbols that come through.

KAMBABA JASPER When you're tuned
in psychically, it's important to stay grounded
so you can remain balanced. Kambaba Jasper
strengthens the connection between your
physical body and your spiritual body so that
you're able to bring the spiritual guidance you
receive back into the physical plane, where you
can decipher it and put it to good use.

During the *Alder Moon*, light some incense—frankincense, jasmine, patchouli, or sandalwood are great options—and make yourself comfortable in your sacred space. Place an Azurite crystal over your Third Eye and close your eyes. Be open to any messages, words, or symbols that enter your mind. When you're ready, hold the stone in your hands to determine the meaning of whatever you received.

The Willow Moon

The Willow Moon is named for the willow tree from the month of May in the Celtic Ogham tree calendar. It's connected to friendship, intellect, the water element, dreams, healing, growth, peace, magic, fertility, knowledge, wishes, success, femininity, and inner vision.

ALTERNATE NAMES Bright Time Moon, Dyan Moon, Moon of Balance, Saille Moon, Simivision Moon, Witches' Moon

ANIMALS bull, cow, snowy owl

COLORS silver, white, yellow

CRYSTALS Angel Aura Quartz, Golden Tiger's Eye, Mangano Calcite

DEITIES Brigit, Cernunnos, Cerridwen, the Green Man

ESSENTIAL OILS blue tansy, carrot seed, vanilla

HERBS bay laurel, coriander, turmeric

KEYWORDS emotions, flexibility, patience

ANGEL AURA QUARTZ Angel Aura Quartz calms your mind and instills patience. Next time you're feeling frustrated, rushed, or overwhelmed, reach for this stone and notice how quickly your energy shifts. It calls in angels, spirit guides, and totem animals to assist you. Add a piece to your altar or medicine pouch to keep its supportive energy handy at all times.

GOLDEN TIGER'S EYE Willow trees' flexibility means they can endure a lot, because they bend and sway instead of breaking. Golden Tiger's Eye also embodies this property and reminds you to be flexible when things don't seem to be going your way. It also reminds you to be flexible when you can't seem to see eye to eye with others. It's important to choose your battles and not waste your energy on things that don't deserve it. If you find yourself getting wrapped up in little things, reach for this stone to remind you about when to flex and when to stand firm.

MANGANO CALCITE This pastel pink stone is opaque and often has faint bands on its surface. Work with it any time your emotions feel high, low, or just plain scattered, to bring you back into balance. Mangano Calcite helps you find your equilibrium, even during difficult times.

Make yourself a medicine bag on the evening of the *Willow Moon*. Include an Angel Aura Quartz, Golden Tiger's Eye, and/or Mangano Calcite along with a written affirmation. This may be something like, "I embody the spirit of the willow; I bend and flex but do not break." Or it may be anything else related to patience, emotional balance, or flexibility. Carry this with you when you're feeling stressed or stretched too thin.

During the *Hawthorn Moon*, draw a Vesica Pisces shape on a piece of paper. Label one circle "Feminine" and one "Masculine." Place a Chrysocolla stone in the feminine circle and a Shiva Lingam stone in the masculine circle. Where the circles overlap, write something you'd like to conceive or birth into the world. Place a Rhodochrosite stone atop the words in this area, and hold space for it to manifest by meditating with it a few times per week.

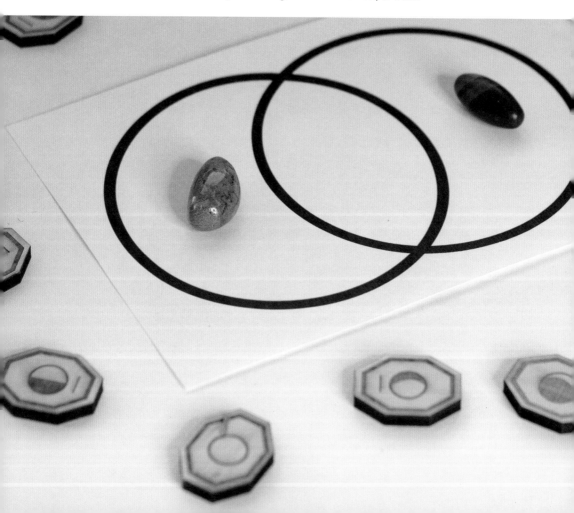

JUNE
The Hawthorn Moon

The Hawthorn Moon is so named because it corresponds to the hawthorn tree from the month of June in the Celtic Ogham tree calendar. It is connected to business, passion, success and luck, calming, forgiveness, the fire element, love and sexuality, the Faeries, change and transformation, positivity, cleansing, creativity, and masculinity.

ALTERNATE NAMES Equos Moon, Horse Time Moon, Huath Moon, Moon of Restraint, Quickest Moon, Thorn-Apple Moon

ANIMALS bee, blackbird, martin

COLORS indigo, lavender, purple

CRYSTALS Chrysocolla, Rhodochrosite, Shiva Lingam

DEITIES Aine, Blodeuwedd, Epona, Etain, Olwyn

ESSENTIAL OILS lotus, vetiver, ylang

HERBS cedar, passion flower, rosemary

KEYWORDS abundance, fertility, triumph

CHRYSOCOLLA Chrysocolla is traditionally known as a goddess energy stone, so it works well to balance the powerful masculine energy of the Hawthorn Moon. This stone enhances abundance in all forms, but it is especially helpful for creating an abundance of new opportunities in life. What is the universe offering you right now? Chrysocolla helps you recognize the new opportunities that await you and nudges you to make positive changes if you feel stuck or scared to move forward—especially if you have a fear of failure.

RHODOCHROSITE This vibrant stone displays contrasting bands of pink and white, and it is connected to the womb. It has associations with fertility and abundance, and it makes a great companion during the time of the Hawthorn Moon. If there's something new you're ready to conceive or birth into the world, now is the time. Rhodochrosite can help.

SHIVA LINGAM Shiva Lingam embraces the masculine energy of this moon. A phallic symbol, the Lingam is a stone of success and triumph, especially in your career or business. The success this stone creates naturally leads to more abundance that will likely show up in your life between the time of the Hawthorn Moon and the Oak Moon in July.

The Oak Moon

The Oak Moon is so named because it corresponds to the oak tree from the month of July in the Celtic Ogham tree calendar. It connects to luck, healing, family and ancestors, heroism, happiness, knowledge and wisdom, longevity, vitality, dreams, fertility, communication, money, and success.

ALTERNATE NAMES Bear Moon, Claiming Time Moon, Duir Moon, Herb Moon, Moon of Security, Moon of Strength

ANIMALS horse, otter, snake

COLORS black, brown, gold

CRYSTALS Hematite, Petrified Wood, Smoky Quartz

DEITIES Cerridwen, the Dagda, the Green Man, Lugh

ESSENTIAL OILS copaiba, palo santo, ravensara

HERBS melissa, oregano, Scotch pine

KEYWORDS protection, stability, strength

HEMATITE Oak is known for being a strong, deeply rooted tree that withstands almost anything. Hematite is quite similar. It's composed mostly of iron, so it's known for being a durable stone. Hematite also has a reputation for being highly protective; it shields the user from negative energy. Work with this stone when you need to draw on its strength or when you know you'll face a difficult encounter.

PETRIFIED WOOD Petrified Wood is created when minerals replace the organic molecules in the plant material. This stone is incredibly grounding and works to enhance stability, both physical and emotional. It also creates more stability in your life—from your career and home life to your spiritual practice and connection with nature. Petrified Wood embodies the energy of the Oak Moon and calls forth the energy of this mighty tree to lend its strength in times of need.

SMOKY QUARTZ This crystal is grounding, but also highly protective. It works to get your attention by alerting your intuition when you're in a situation or an environment that's not for your highest good (e.g., when you're surrounded by people who are draining your energy, in a space with bad vibes that don't align with your energy, or just not honoring your true self).

On the evening of the *Oak Moon*, place a Smoky Quartz crystal on your altar and tune into the energy of the crystal. Breathe in and out, and allow your breath to surround the stone. Ask the stone to alert you when you're in any situation where there are negative vibes and protection is needed. Carry your stone with you for protective support.

To connect with the energy of the *Holly Moon*, place a Bloodstone in a jar of water and cover it with a lid. Set the jar outside overnight on the evening of the Holly Moon. The next morning, pour the charged water into a spray bottle and use it for cleansing your space, your aura, and your crystals.

The Holly Moon

The Holly Moon is named for the holly bush from the month of August in the Celtic Ogham tree calendar. It's connected to justice, protection, healing, leadership and confidence, balance, mental clarity, generosity, masculine energy, and safe travels.

ALTERNATE NAMES Arbitration Time Moon, Bat's Wings Moon, Dispute Moon, Edrinious Moon, Moon of Encirclement, Tinne Moon

ANIMALS cardinal, goat, starling

COLORS light blue, red, silver

CRYSTALS Bloodstone, Blue Topaz, Ocean Jasper

DEITIES Balor, Gronw Pebr, the Holly King, Lugh, Taranus

HERBS burdock, ginger, nettle

ESSENTIAL OILS clove, lemon, tea tree

KEYWORDS cleansing, purification, renewal

BLOODSTONE Bloodstone is linked to the Holly Moon and even resembles the holly plant. The small red flecks on the dark green body of the stone look like little holly berries on a canopy of leaves. This is a stone of leadership and exudes the masculine energy of the Holly Moon. This moon is linked to the Holly King, who starts rising to power this time of year to take over from the Oak King. Bloodstone aligns your energy with the changing seasons and assists with the slow transition into winter.

BLUE TOPAZ This silvery-blue stone looks like it contains the light of the moon itself. Blue Topaz promotes mental clarity and refreshes you after long periods of stress or fatigue. It's well suited to the Holly Moon because of its ability to renew your energy and rejuvenate your physical being. This crystal helps you wrap up loose ends and finish old projects so that you're able to start anew without any baggage.

OCEAN JASPER This stone, also known as Orbicular Jasper, is from Madagascar, and it is mostly mined from along the shoreline. It has a connection to the water and washes away that which is no longer needed in your life. This brings a sense of renewal to the spirit and creates space for new things to enter your life.

To connect with the energy of the *Hazel Moon*, place a piece of Jet in a bowl of hazelnuts near the main entrance to your home. Hover your hands above the bowl, close your eyes, and visualize the stone glowing with protective energy. See this energy surround the entrance to your home and expand until all doors and windows are glowing with the protective light. Leave it in place to keep your home protected.

The Hazel Moon

The Hazel Moon is so named because it corresponds to the hazel shrub from the month of September in the Celtic Ogham tree calendar. It is connected to the early harvest, manifestation, order, prosperity, love and marriage, communication, knowledge and wisdom, truth and honesty, intuition, the water element, writing and art, creative inspiration, and protection.

ALTERNATE NAMES Cantlos Moon, Coll Moon, Crone Moon, Moon of the Wise, Singing Moon, Song Time Moon

ANIMALS badger, salmon, sheep

COLORS brown, orange, yellow

CRYSTALS Amber, Blue Sapphire, Jet

DEITIES Aengus, Dagda, Danu, Gwydion, Myrrdin, Oghma

HERBS black pepper, sweet marjoram, thyme

ESSENTIAL OILS blue tansy, eucalyptus, myrrh

KEYWORDS awareness, consciousness, understanding

AMBER Amber has ancient associations with magic. Working with this stone during the time of the Hazel Moon opens the mind to new realms of conscious awareness. Historically, people believed this crystal to be fossilized sunlight that draws its power from the Sun. When paired with the lunar energy of the Hazel Moon, Amber brings balance between these energies, resulting in a deep understanding of the ebb and flow of universal energies around you.

BLUE SAPPHIRE This blue variety of Corundum is the traditional birthstone for the month of September. It has been used to stimulate the Third Eye Chakra to awaken dormant intuitive abilities and create a connection to Spirit. Blue Sapphire enhances all spiritual experiences and deepens meditation, especially when the goal of the meditation is expanding the conscious mind.

JET This mineral has long been considered a natural partner to Amber. When used together, the stones create powerful magic. When used during the time of the Hazel Moon, this magic is even more potent. The pair make a powerful duo to assist your manifesting practice. Additionally, Jet is a protective stone and can be used to keep you and your family energetically shielded from negativity.

OCTOBER

The Vine Moon

The Vine Moon is named for the vine from the month of October in the Celtic Ogham tree calendar. It is connected to ambition, gardening, tranquility, compassion and empathy, group cooperation, balance, happiness, celebration, and setting and achieving goals.

ALTERNATE NAMES Bramble Moon, Moon of Celebration, Muin Moon, Muinn Moon, Samonios Moon, Seed-Fall Moon

ANIMALS hare, hawk, swan

COLORS copper, gold, pink

CRYSTALS Blue Chalcedony, Boulder Opal, Copper

DEITIES Anu, Arianrhod, Druantia the Queen of the Druids, Margawse, Nodens, Sucellus

ESSENTIAL OILS palmarosa, peppermint, spruce

HERBS bilberry, comfrey, dandelion

KEYWORDS ambition, charm, pride

BLUE CHALCEDONY Blue Chalcedony has a sweet energy, and it enhances charm and likability. It's a great stone for those who need to work closely with others in a group or assume leadership positions. Further, this crystal helps you keep a cool head in difficult situations or when working with opposing personalities.

BOULDER OPAL This stunning rainbow mineral from Australia displays swirls and sparkles of light that look like starry galaxies trapped in stone. This crystal assists those with ambition in reaching their goals by helping them realize no dream is too big. Nothing is out of reach when you set your mind to it. The Vine Moon is an excellent time for making big strides toward your dreams. Work with Boulder Opal to help you visualize the steps that need to be taken to move you closer toward achieving your goals.

COPPER This orange metal is excellent for promoting self-love. This stone helps you recognize and appreciate your own achievements, taking pride in what you've accomplished. Copper also encourages you to acknowledge where you may have fallen short in the past so that you're able to move past any negativity you may be holding on to about the situation. Once you've released these energy blocks, you can fully embrace even the small wins you have made.

To connect with the energy of the *Vine Moon*, meditate while holding a Boulder Opal up to your Third Eye and think about something very important that you'd like to accomplish in your life—this should be a big soul path goal. Picture all of the steps that you'll need to take to get there and visualize the outcome in as much detail as possible.

The Reed Moon

The Reed Moon is so named because it corresponds to the reed plant from the month of November in the Celtic Ogham tree calendar. It is connected to grounding, meditation, history, love and romance, the underworld, harmony, divination, honor, protection, and spirit guides. It was also known as the Dark Moon, referring to the longer nights as the wheel of the year turns toward deep winter. Another name for the November Moon was the Mourning Moon because the Celtic year ended in October and started anew in November, so we mourn the end of another annual cycle.

ALTERNATE NAMES Dark Moon, Elm Moon, Hearth Moon, Mourning Moon, Ngetal Moon, Riuros Moon

ANIMALS hound, owl, whale

COLORS black, brown, orange

CRYSTALS Bronzite, Dravite Tourmaline, Pietersite

DEITIES Aine, Arawn, Breton, Diancecht, Miach, Nantosuelta

ESSENTIAL OILS jasmine, lemongrass, vetiver

HERBS chamomile, nettle, sweet birch

KEYWORDS evolution, healing, life cycles

BRONZITE This brown stone displays copper-colored, flashy flecks. It encourages a return to nature and nudges you to live in balance with the cycles of nature. Bronzite helps you relax into the ebb and flow of the year and prepare for the darkness of winter. Take this time to retreat inward and focus on self-care. Let Bronzite help you with deep healing.

DRAVITE TOURMALINE Also known as Champagne Tourmaline, this brown crystal is highly protective. It promotes healing of the physical body, and it balances the energy of the aura and chakra centers. Dravite Tourmaline aligns the physical, emotional, mental, and spiritual bodies. It also enhances your ability to connect with the healing energy of plants and can enhance studies related to herbalism and natural medicines.

PIETERSITE This lesser-known stone from South Africa has an intense energy that promotes the expansion of consciousness. Pietersite can be used to enhance meditation, astral travel, shamanic journeying, psychic readings, and other high-vibrational work.

To connect with the energy of the *Reed Moon*, brew a mug of chamomile tea and create a triangular-shaped crystal grid around the cup using one each of Bronzite, Dravite Tourmaline, and Pietersite. Let the tea charge in the grid while it cools. Then sip the tea while intending to fill your being with healing energy and aligning yourself with the cycles of nature.

To connect with the energy of the *Elder Moon*, wear a piece of Sodalite or Aquamarine jewelry. When you feel overwhelmed, bring your attention to the stone, close your eyes, and focus on your breath. Breathe in for a count of four, and exhale for a count of four. This deep, rhythmic breathing will bring you back to center and create stillness in your mind.

The Elder Moon

The Elder Moon is so named because it corresponds to the elder tree from the month of December in the Celtic Ogham tree calendar. It is connected to creativity, kindness, renewal and rejuvenation, freedom, mediumship and seership, prosperity, nature spirits, new beginnings, and protection.

ALTERNATE NAMES Lady Ellhorn Moon, Moon of Completeness, Old Gal Moon, Old Lady Moon, Ruis Moon, Ruish Moon

ANIMALS bull, fox, pheasant

COLORS black, dark green, gold

CRYSTALS Lepidolite, Shungite, Sodalite

DEITIES Cailleach, Dagda, the Green Man, the Holly King, the White Lady

ESSENTIAL OILS chamomile, rosemary, sage

HERBS garlic, hyssop, oregano

KEYWORDS grounding, rest, stillness

LEPIDOLITE The Elder Moon is a time for rest and rejuvenation. Lepidolite is aligned with this energy due to its ability to quiet the mind and create stillness in your inner world. This crystal works well to calm an anxious mind, especially when paired with Aquamarine. Wear it as a piece of jewelry during the time of the Elder Moon—or any time, really—for a reminder to center yourself and focus on the present moment.

SHUNGITE Shungite is an excellent grounding stone, and because of its high vibration, it has a way of bringing your spiritual body down into the physical plane so that you can integrate wisdom and lessons from the universe. A powerful cleanser, this crystal can help you banish things from your life that are draining your energy so that you can rest without the chaos of those things weighing you down and drawing your attention away from rejuvenation.

SODALITE This indigo stone helps you turn inward and create calm stillness in your inner world even if the world around you seems to be in disarray. Sodalite reminds you that you are your own sacred space and that you can create your own reality if you so choose.

On the evening of the *Ivy Moon*, place a photo of yourself on your altar and set a Black Onyx stone atop it. Light a black candle, for protection, and ask that the universe keep you shielded from any energies that are not for your highest good. Repeat this ritual each Ivy (Blue) Moon for lasting protection until the next Ivy Moon.

BLUE

The Ivy Moon

The Ivy Moon is so named because it corresponds to the ivy vine from the extra moon in the Celtic Ogham tree calendar. It is connected to friendship, cycles of birth and death, release, generosity, rebirth, faith, the shadow side, determination and productivity, and breaking old habits.

ALTERNATE NAMES Dummanios Moon, Gort Moon, Mid Samonios Moon, Moon of Buoyancy, Moon of Resilience

ANIMALS duck, porpoise, swan

COLORS blue, light yellow, white

CRYSTALS Black Onyx, Charoite, White Pearl

DEITIES Caer Ibormeith, Dewi, Epona, Llew Llaw Gyffes, Llyr, Nechtan

ESSENTIAL OILS oregano, peppermint, rosemary

HERBS catmint, chicory, woolly thyme

KEYWORDS love, protection, triumph

BLACK ONYX This black variety of Chalcedony is an excellent stone for leaders. It works well for those who must manage a team in a cooperative project and increases the chances of a successful outcome. Black Onyx is highly protective and will help shield you from outside energies that are not for your highest good. Work with this crystal when success and triumph are very important, and call upon the universe for support.

CHAROITE This swirling purple, pearlescent stone comes from Russia and is highly sought after for its intense color. It's a stone of love in its purest form, promoting the unconditional love of all beings. Charoite also promotes divine love and enhances your connection to Spirit. Further, it's a useful crystal if you have a hard time keeping one foot in the physical realm and often feel disconnected from your body.

WHITE PEARL Before cultured Pearls were commercially available, these tiny spheres were prized for their rarity. White Pearls look like tiny, glowing moons and have been associated with the moon and lunar energies since ancient times. The spherical shape of these gemstones represents wholeness and completion. For this reason, they make excellent symbols of enduring love and friendship.

Glossary

AFFIRMATION An empowering statement rooted in positive thinking that supports personal growth and enhances the ability to manifest.

ALL THAT IS Everything in the universe, both known and unknown.

ANGELS High-energy messengers of light that can be called upon to help you with your day-to-day life.

ARCHETYPE A concept representative of a specific idea, belief system, behavioral pattern, personality type, or way of being that rests within the mass consciousness; may be associated with cultural or societal symbols to represent different aspects of human nature.

ASTRAL TRAVEL The act of journeying to alternate times and places using the astral body (also known as the energy body), typically during the dream state; a willful out-of-body experience.

ASTROLOGICAL HOUSE One of twelve segments of the Zodiac; each is ruled by a different astrological sign and relates to specific areas of life. These are determined by the time, date, and location of an event (usually a person's birth).

AURA The subtle energy field surrounding all living things.

BLACK MOON Traditionally the second new moon in a given calendar month, but also sometimes used to describe a month with no full moon or the second full moon in a calendar month.

BLOOD MOON The name given to the moon when it appears reddish in color, during a lunar eclipse, due to the way the Sun's light passes around the edges of the Earth, through part of the Earth's atmosphere.

BLUE MOON Traditionally, the name given to the fourth full moon in a quarter (a three-month period), but also used to describe the second full moon in a given calendar month.

CENTERING The process of turning inward and focusing the conscious mind on present-moment awareness.

CHAKRA Spinning vortices of energy found in the aura, corresponding with different parts of the physical body, sets of emotions, and aspects of the spirit. There are typically thought to be seven major chakras and many other minor chakras in the energy body.

CHARGING The process of replenishing an object's universal energy.

CLAIRAUDIENCE A type of psychic skill that allows someone with this gift to hear messages or information from the subtle realms.

CLAIRVOYANCE A type of psychic skill that allows someone with this gift to see energy from the subtle realms that provides information or messages.

CLEANSING The process of removing energy that's not for the highest good of those involved from an object or an environment.

CRYSTAL Refers to any mineral with a regularly repeating atomic structure (a crystalline blueprint). Crystals are formed from building-block-like units of matter, and the physical appearance of the crystal often reflects its internal molecular arrangement.

DEITY A sacred being often considered divine in nature; people of most faiths and religious paths incorporate at least one deity into their spiritual practice.

DIVINATION A form of gaining knowledge of the future or insight into a particular issue or question by means of ritual, omens, and/or psychic skills. Information is typically received in signs or symbols, and it must be interpreted by the diviner by way of their intuition.

DREAMWORK The act of healing or personal exploration from within the dream state.

ELEMENT A reference to the classical, Greek elements of earth, air, fire, water, and ether, thought in ancient times to be the building blocks of everything within the universe. Each is thought to correspond to specific archetypal energies, body parts, emotions, Zodiac signs, and more.

ESSENTIAL OIL A concentrated substance of aromatic compounds made by distilling various plants; they're extremely fragrant and are used in aromatherapy and other forms of alternative medicine.

FIRST QUARTER MOON The point at which the moon is one-quarter of the way through the lunar cycle (halfway between the new moon and the full moon), when the moon is 50% lighted in its right side.

FULL MOON The halfway point in the lunar cycle, when the moon is completely lighted.

GRID A geometrically arranged group of crystals intentionally placed in a sacred space to affect the flow of energy for a specific purpose or intention.

GROUNDING The process of connecting the subtle energy of the body with the energy of the Earth to provide protection, healing, and balance.

HERB A medicinal, healing plant.

HIGHER SELF The part of a person or their spirit that represents their most perfect, whole, and authentic self.

HIGHEST GOOD That which is in the best interest of all involved.

INNER SELF The part of a person that represents their innermost, subconscious self.

INTENTION STATEMENT A goal-focused affirmation related to something you wish to manifest or attract into your life.

INTUITION Inner knowing; insight gained through the subconscious mind rather than through the rational mind.

LAST QUARTER MOON The point at which the moon is three-quarters of the way through the lunar cycle (halfway between the full moon and the next new moon) where the moon is 50% lighted in its left side.

LENORMAND An early form of French cartomancy divination named for the famous fortune-teller Marie Anne Lenormand; it used a deck of playing cards (or sometimes just a specific portion of a deck).

LIGHTWORKER A person who supports the spiritual evolution of all beings. These people always act for the highest good of all.

LUCID DREAMING A type of dreaming wherein the dreamer is aware that they are in the dream state; also called conscious dreaming.

LUNAR ECLIPSE An event where some or all of a full moon appears dark; it occurs when the Earth is directly between the Sun and the moon and the Earth casts a shadow on the moon's surface.

MANIFESTING The act of attracting something into your life through the use of intention, affirmations, or other positive means.

MEDICINE POUCH A small bag traditionally filled with meaningful, healing objects used for personal empowerment; it's considered very sacred.

MEDITATION The act of reaching a perfect stillness of mind through inner reflection or guided visualization.

MICRO MOON The term used to describe the moon when it's at its furthest orbital point from the Earth; opposite of a Super Moon. Also called an Apogee Moon or a Mini Moon.

MOON PHASE One of eight distinct periods during the lunar cycle characterized by the amount of the sunlight being reflected by the moon's surface.

NEW MOON The first point in the lunar cycle at which the moon is completely dark.

OGHAM A Celtic alphabet derived from tree archetypes that was used to write an early form of the Irish language.

PALO SANTO The wood of a sacred tree from Peru, known as Holy Wood, that's burned as a cleansing incense.

PINEAL GLAND A small, conical, endocrine gland located near the center of the brain. It's connected to the Third Eye Chakra, and it can be activated during meditation.

PROGRAMMING The act of purposefully storing an intention or affirmation within a crystal so that the stone may amplify your thought form and assist you with manifesting.

PSYCHIC SKILLS Extrasensory abilities that may be used to gain insight, knowledge, or messages from the subtle realms; this includes clairvoyance and clairaudience, among others.

RITUAL A spiritual practice that requires steps or actions to be performed in a specific order.

RULING PLANET In astrology, the classical planet corresponding to each individual sign that has the strongest influence over that sign. A planet may rule one or more signs.

SACRED GEOMETRY The idea that specific geometric shapes hold energetic vibrations and correspond to specific attributes or universal truths.

SACRED SPACE Your personal, spiritual sanctuary; the space where you can connect to universal energy for healing, balance, meditation, ritual, and more.

SAGE An herb of the *Salvia* genus burned as a powerful cleansing incense. The smoke is used to purify the energy of people, places, and objects.

SCRYING Any form of divination in which a person gazes into an object or substance to receive visions and guidance. Commonly performed with bowls of water or with crystal balls.

SHAMAN A special kind of healer who can connect with spirits and the subtle energy realms; may perform healing work, ritual, divination, or other rites.

SHAMANIC JOURNEY A physical or mental journey undertaken by someone practicing shamanism that leads them to other realms where wisdom and insight may be gathered about a particular issue, illness, mental state, or other problem.

SHIELDING The act of protecting the self or the environment from negative energy (energy that's not for the highest good) by means of an energetic barrier.

SMUDGING The act of cleansing and purifying a person, place, or object with the smoke given off by burning any number of sacred herbs; sage, palo santo, and cedar are most commonly used.

SPIRIT GUIDES High-vibrational beings who act as personal guides or teachers; they may offer you information or messages, protection, healing, and more.

SUPER MOON The term used to describe the moon when it's at its closest orbital point to the Earth. It is the opposite of a Micro Moon. Also called a Perigee Moon.

TAROT A form of cartomancy divination that uses tarot cards. A standard tarot deck contains 78 total cards. It includes 22 Major Arcana (Trump) cards that do not have suits but represent different archetypal energies. It also includes 56 Minor Arcana cards divided into 4 suits of 14 cards each. Suits traditionally include wands, cups, pentacles, and swords, but they may vary from deck to deck depending upon the creator's preference.

TOTEM ANIMAL A special animal spirit guide or an animal you see frequently in nature that acts as a signal for energies the universe is sharing with you.

WANING CRESCENT MOON The period in the lunar cycle where the moon is between the last quarter moon phase and the next new moon phase. The moon is partially (1% to 49%) lighted on the left side.

WANING GIBBOUS MOON The period in the lunar cycle where the moon is between the full moon phase and the last quarter moon phase. The moon is partially (51% to 99%) lighted on the left side.

WAXING CRESCENT MOON The period in the lunar cycle where the moon is between the new moon phase and the first quarter moon phase. The moon is partially (1% to 49%) lighted on the right side.

WAXING GIBBOUS MOON The period in the lunar cycle where the moon is between the first quarter moon phase and the full moon phase. The moon is partially (51% to 99%) lighted on the right side.

ZODIAC The area of the sky surrounding the Sun's ecliptic that is divided into the twelve astrological signs (represented by classic mythical animals and archetypes).

Further Reading

BOOKS

Ahlquist, Diane. *Moon Magic: Your Complete Guide to Harnessing the Mystical Energy of the Moon.* Avon, MA: Adams Media, 2017.

Ahlquist, Diane. *Moon Spells: How to Use the Moon to Get What You Want.* Avon, MA: Adams Media, 2002.

Boland, Yasmin. *Moonology: Working with the Magic of the Lunar Cycles.* Carlsbad, CA: Hay House, 2016.

Briggs, Viktorija. *A Witch's Craft Volume 2: A Witch's Book of Correspondences.* Midnight Blue Publishing, 2016.

Butler, Simone. *Moon Power: Lunar Rituals for Connecting with Your Inner Goddess.* Beverly, MA: Fair Winds Press, 2017.

Conway, D.J. *Moon Magick: Myth & Magick, Crafts & Recipes, Rituals & Spells.* Woodbury, MN: Llewellyn Publications, 2017.

Morrison, Dorothy. *Moon Magic: Spells & Rituals for Abundant Living.* Woodbury, MN: Llewellyn Publications, 2017.

Robbins, Heather Roan. *Moon Wisdom: Transform Your Life Using the Moon's Signs and Cycles.* New York: Cico Books, 2015.

Spencer, Ezzie. *Lunar Abundance: Cultivating Joy, Peace, and Purpose Using the Phases of the Moon.* New York: Running Press, 2018.

WEBSITES

Act for Libraries
www.actforlibraries.org

Ancient-Wisdom
www.ancient-wisdom.com

Anne Beversdorf: Stariel Astrology
www.stariel.com

Astro Theme
www.astrotheme.com

Cafe Astrology
www.cafeastrology.com

Coven Life
www.covenlife.co

EarthSky
www.earthsky.org

Eco Enchantments
www.ecoenchantments.co.uk

Farmers' Almanac
www.farmersalmanac.com

The Goddess Tree
www.thegoddesstree.com

Historyplex
www.historyplex.com

The Irish News
www.irishnews.com

Joelle's Sacred Grove
www.joellessacredgrove.com

Living Myths
www.livingmyths.com

MoonCircles
www.mooncircles.com

MoonConnection.com
www.moonconnection.com

Moon Giant
www.moongiant.com

Mystic Mamma
www.mysticmamma.com

Native Languages of the Americas
www.native-languages.org

The Old Farmer's Almanac
www.almanac.com

The Pagans Path
www.paganspath.com

Patheos: Beneath the Moon
www.patheos.com/blogs/beneaththemoon

Sky & Telescope
www.skyandtelescope.com

The Smart Witch
www.thesmartwitch.com

ThoughtCo.
www.thoughtco.com

Timeanddate.com
www.timeanddate.com

Western Washington University: Skywise Unlimited
www.wwu.edu/skywise

Whats-Your-Sign.com
www.whats-your-sign.com

Photograph by Arturo Aguilar, www.arturoaguilarphoto.com

About the Author

ASHLEY LEAVY is one of the world's top crystal experts and educators. Over the past decade, she has helped tens of thousands of people discover the power of crystals for healing and transformation. Ashley's passion for crystal healing has attracted notice from the media, and her work has been featured in hundreds of magazines, newspapers, blogs, TV programs, podcasts, and radio shows.

As the founder and educational director of the Love & Light School of Crystal Therapy, Ashley has created dozens of online courses for anyone interested in learning more about crystals, including a comprehensive, award-winning Crystal Healing Certification Program. With classes that are fun, educational, and life-transforming, the Love & Light School has quickly grown into a thriving international community of heart-centered healers and energy workers—at both the hobbyist and the professional level. Whether you're new to crystal healing or an experienced practitioner looking for advanced techniques to grow your practice, the Love & Light School offers a broad range of training programs to support you in creating a life that's in alignment with your soul's purpose. Learn more at www.LoveAndLightSchool.com.

In addition to teaching, Ashley owns a popular New Age store in Madison, Wisconsin, called Mimosa Books & Gifts. You can follow it on Instagram @MimosaSpirit. Ashley has published numerous books on crystals as well as the Crystal Moon Mystic Oracle Deck.

When she isn't working with students, behind the desk at Mimosa, or writing, you'll usually find Ashley traveling, spending time in nature, or fundraising for local animal shelters and rescues.

Are you curious about using crystals to make positive changes for yourself? For some free crystal healing gifts, visit Ashley's website: www.LoveAndLightSchool.com/gifts or follow her on Instagram @LoveAndLightSchool.

About the Photographer

JENNIFER ANN is an intuitive design alchemist. She's a Gulf Coast native who is obsessed with natural health, nature, beauty, and all things awakening to the soul. Jennifer specializes in creating sacred designs and photography for female entrepreneurs to help them express their soul gifts with heart and soul.

Index

Adularia, 49
Alder Moon, 164–165
Amazonite, 86, 87
Amber
    Hazel Moon, 175
    Strawberry Moon, 140
Amethyst
    full moon, 44
    Ice Moon, 104
    Storm Moon, 107
Angel Aura Quartz, 166, 167
Angelite
    Cancer Moon, 71
    first quarter moon, 41
    sacred space and, 15
Apache Tear, 66
Apogee Full Moon, 57
Apricot Botswana Agate, 52, 53
Apricot Moonstone, 115
April
    Alder Moon, 164–165
    Fish Moon, 136–137
    Growing Moon, 108–109
Aqua Aura Quartz, 86
Aquamarine
    Elder Moon, 180
    Long Nights Moon, 152, 153
    sacred space and, 15
    waning gibbous moon, 49
Aquarius, 84–85
Aragonite, 160, 161
Aries, 64–65
Ash Moon, 162–163
August
    Corn Moon, 116–117
    Grain Moon, 144–145
    Holly Moon, 172–173
Auralite-23, 164
Azure Moon, 154–155
Azurite
    Alder Moon, 164, 165
    Libra Moon, 77

Beaver Moon, 150–151
Biggs Picture Jasper, 143
Birch Moon, 158–159
Black Moons, 56, 98

Black Moonstone
    new moon, 34, 35–36
    waning crescent moon, 52
    waxing crescent moon, 39
    Wolf Moon, 102, 103
Black Obsidian
    Scorpio Moon, 79
    waning gibbous moon, 48, 49
Black Onyx, 182, 183
Black Opal, 79
Black Tourmaline
    Crow Moon, 134, 135
    energy clearing, 19
    grounding exercise, 20
Blood Moon, 55, 120–121
Bloodstone
    Blood Moon, 120, 121
    Holly Moon, 172, 173
Blue Apatite
    Crow Moon, 134, 135
    Gemini Moon, 68, 69
Blue Calcite
    Growing Moon, 109
    waning crescent moon, 52
Blue Chalcedony
    Old Moon, 130
    Vine Moon, 176
Blue Fluorite, 84
Blue Kyanite, 155
Blue Lace Agate
    Aquarius Moon, 84
    Blue Moon, 126, 127
    waxing gibbous moon, 42
Blue Moons
    Azure Moon, 154–155
    Blue Moon, 126–127
    introduction, 98
    Ivy Moon, 182–183
Blue Quartz, 126
Blue Sapphire
    Hazel Moon, 175
    Libra Moon, 77
Blue Topaz, 173
Boulder Opal, 176, 177
Bronzite, 178, 179
Buck Moon, 142–143
Buddstone, 82, 83

Cancer, 70–71
Capricorn, 82–83
Carnelian
    Corn Moon, 116, 117
    energy clearing, 19
    first quarter moon, 41
Celestite
    Aquarius Moon, 84, 85
    Hunter's Moon, 148, 149
Celtic Moons
    Alder Moon, 164–165
    Ash Moon, 162–163
    Birch Moon, 158–159
    Elder Moon, 180–181
    Hawthorn Moon, 168–169
    Hazel Moon, 174–175
    Holly Moon, 172–173
    introduction, 97
    Ivy Moon, 182–183
    Oak Moon, 170–171
    Reed Moon, 178–179
    Rowan Moon, 160–161
    Vine Moon, 176–177
    Willow Moon, 166–167
centering, 21, 22
Charoite, 183
Chrysanthemum Stone, 132, 133
Chrysocolla, 168, 169
Chrysoprase, 108, 109
Citrine
    Harvest Moon, 118, 119
    Rose Moon, 112
    Sagittarius Moon, 80
    waxing gibbous moon, 42, 43
cleansing
    crystals, 16, 22
    objects, 16
    smudging, 16, 17
    spaces, 16, 17
clearing, 18
Clear Quartz
    Ice Moon, 104, 105
    last quarter moon, 50
    Snow Moon, 122, 123
Coffee Moonstone, 42
Cold Moon, 124–125
Connemara Marble, 159

Copper, 176
Corn Moon, 116–117
Crow Moon, 134–135

Danburite, 72, 73
December
    Cold Moon, 124–125
    Elder Moon, 180–181
    Long Nights Moon, 152–153
Diamond, 132
Dravite Tourmaline, 178, 179
Dumortierite, 124

eclipses, 55
Elder Moon, 180–181
Emerald
    Birch Moon, 159
    Hare Moon, 110
    Virgo Moon, 74, 75
Ethiopian Opal, 123

February
    Frost Moon, 132–133
    Ice Moon, 104–105
    Rowan Moon, 160–161
Fire Agate, 73
Fire Opal, 115
first quarter moon, 32, 40–41, 46
Fish Moon, 136–137
Flower Moon, 138–139
Frost Moon, 132–133
Fruit Moon, 146–147
full moons, 44–46, 90–91

Gemini, 68–69
Golden Tiger's Eye
    Leo Moon, 73
    new moon, 34–35, 36
    Willow Moon, 166, 167
Grain Moon, 144–145
Green Aventurine
    Ash Moon, 162, 163
    Virgo Moon, 74
    waxing crescent moon, 38, 39
Green Grossular Garnet, 144
Green Jadeite Jade, 118, 119

Green Nephrite Jade
    Growing Moon, 109
    waxing crescent
        moon, 38
grounding, 20, 22

Hare Moon, 110–111
Harvest Moon, 90–91,
    118–119
Hawthorn Moon, 168–169
Hazel Moon, 174–175
healing crystals, 12–13
Heliodor
    Flower Moon, 139
    Grain Moon, 144
Hematite, 170
Hessonite Garnet, 152
Holly Moon, 172–173
Honey Calcite, 112
Howlite
    Birch Moon, 158, 159
    Gemini Moon, 68, 69
Hunter's Moon, 148–149

Ice Moon, 104–105
Imperial Topaz, 80, 81
inspiration, 25
intention, 22
Iolite, 143
Ivy Moon, 182–183

jade
    Green Jadeite Jade,
        118, 119
    Green Nephrite Jade,
        38, 109
January
    Birch Moon, 158–159
    Old Moon, 130
    Wolf Moon, 102–103
Jet
    Hazel Moon, 174, 175
    Scorpio Moon, 78, 79
July
    Buck Moon, 142–143
    Hay Moon, 114–115
    Oak Moon, 170–171
June
    Hawthorn Moon,
        168–169
    Rose Moon, 112–113
    Strawberry Moon,
        140–141

Kambaba Jasper, 164

Labradorite
    full moons, 44–45
    Wolf Moon, 102, 103
Lapis Lazuli
    Cold Moon, 124
    Sagittarius Moon, 80
    waning gibbous
        moon, 49
Larimar
    Cancer Moon, 70, 71
    Fish Moon, 137
    Pisces Moon, 86
last quarter moon, 46,
    50–51
Lava Rock, 65
Leo, 72–73
Lepidolite, 181
Libra, 76–77
Lodestone, 107
Long Nights Moon,
    152–153
lunar cycles
    alignment, 33
    Apogee Full Moon, 57
    Black Moons, 56
    Blood Moons, 55
    eclipses, 55
    first quarter moon, 32,
        40–41, 46
    full moons, 44–46,
        90–91
    introduction, 31–33
    last quarter moon, 46,
        50–51
    Lunar Zodiac, 60–61
    Micro Moons, 57
    new moons, 32,
        34–36, 46
    Perigee Full Moon, 57
    Super Moons, 57
    waning moons, 32, 46,
        48–49, 52–53, 53
    waxing moons, 32,
        38–39, 42–43, 46
lunar energy
    amplification, 27
    history, 26
    inspiration, 25
    overview, 24
Lunar Zodiac
    introduction, 60
    lunar cycle and, 60–61
    moon calendars and,
        60–61

Mangano Calcite, 166, 167
March
    Ash Moon, 162–163
    Crow Moon, 134–135
    Storm Moon, 106–107
May
    Flower Moon, 138–139
    Hare Moon, 110–111
    Willow Moon, 166–167
Micro Moons, 57
Modern Moons
    Blood Moon, 120–121
    Blue Moon, 126–127
    Cold Moon, 124–125
    Corn Moon, 116–117
    Growing Moon,
        108–109
    Hare Moon, 110–111
    Harvest Moon, 90–91,
        118–119
    Hay Moon, 114–115
    Ice Moon, 104–105
    introduction, 92
    Rose Moon, 112–113
    Snow Moon, 91,
        122–123
    Storm Moon, 106–107
    Wolf Moon, 102–103
Mookaite Jasper, 140, 141
moon calendars, 60–61
moon signs
    Aquarius, 84–85
    Aries, 64–65
    Cancer, 70–71
    Capricorn, 82–83
    Gemini, 68–69
    introduction, 61–62
    Leo, 72–73
    Libra, 76–77
    lunar zodiac, 62
    Pisces, 86–87
    Sagittarius, 62, 80–81
    Scorpio, 78–79
    Taurus, 62, 66–67
    Virgo, 74–75
Morganite, 163
Moss Agate, 74, 75

Native Moons
    Azure Moon, 154–155
    Beaver Moon, 150–151
    Buck Moon, 142–143
    Crow Moon, 134–135
    Fish Moon, 136–137
    Flower Moon, 138–139

Frost Moon, 132–133
    Fruit Moon, 146–147
    Grain Moon, 144–145
    Hunter's Moon,
        148–149
    introduction, 95
    Long Nights Moon,
        152–153
    Old Moon, 130–131
    Strawberry Moon,
        140–141
new moons, 32, 34–36, 46
November
    Beaver Moon, 150–151
    Reed Moon, 178–179
    Snow Moon, 122–123

Oak Moon, 170–171
object cleansing, 16
Ocean Jasper, 173
October
    Blood Moon, 120–121
    Hunter's Moon,
        148–149
    Vine Moon, 176–177
Old Moon, 130–131
oracle cards, 45–46
Orange Calcite, 118, 119

Peach Aventurine, 116
Peach Moonstone
    last quarter moon,
        50, 51
    Old Moon, 130
Peach Selenite, 152
Peridot, 139
Perigee Full Moon, 57
Petrified Wood
    Beaver Moon, 151
    grounding, 20
    Oak Moon, 170
Pietersite, 178, 179
Pink Aventurine, 132
Pink Opal, 66
Pink Spinel, 155
Pink Stilbite, 163
Pink Tourmaline
    Blood Moon, 120
    Storm Moon, 106, 107
Pisces, 86–87
Pruett, James Hugh, 98
Pyrite
    Fruit Moon, 146, 147
    last quarter moon,
        50, 51

quarter moons. *See* first
quarter moon; last
quarter moon.
quartz
   Angel Aura Quartz,
   166, 167
   Blue Quartz, 126
   Clear Quartz, 50, 104,
   105, 122, 123
   Rose Quartz, 15, 19, 41,
   66, 67, 104, 110, 111,
   112, 113
   Rutilated Quartz,
   114, 115
   Smoky Quartz, 82, 83,
   170, 171
   Strawberry Quartz, 140

Rainbow Fluorite
   Crow Moon, 134, 135
   Libra Moon, 76, 77
Rainbow Moonstone
   Blue Moon, 126
   Cancer Moon, 71
   full moons, 45
   new moons, 35, 36
Rainbow Sheen Obsidian,
150, 151
Rainforest Jasper
   Capricorn Moon, 82, 83
   Flower Moon, 138, 139
Red Calcite, 146, 147
Red Garnet, 65
Red Jasper, 148, 149
Red Pyrope Garnet,
142, 143
Red Spinel, 160
Reed Moon, 178–179
Rhodochrosite
   Fish Moon, 136, 137
   Hawthorn Moon, 168,
   169
   last quarter moon, 50
Rhodonite
   Hare Moon, 110
   lunar cycles, 35

rituals
   Alder Moon, 165
   Aquarius Moon, 85
   Aries Moon, 64
   Ash Moon, 162
   Blood Moon, 121
   Blue Moon, 127
   Buck Moon, 142
   Cancer Moon, 70
   Capricorn Moon, 82
   centering, 21
   Cold Moon, 125
   Corn Moon, 117
   Elder Moon, 180
   Fish Moon, 136
   Flower Moon, 138
   Frost Moon, 133
   Fruit Moon, 147
   full moon, 45–46
   Gemini Moon, 68
   Grain Moon, 145
   grounding, 20
   Growing Moon, 108
   Hare Moon, 111
   Harvest Moon, 118
   Hawthorn Moon, 168
   Hay Moon, 114
   Hazel Moon, 174
   Holly Moon, 172
   Hunter's Moon, 148
   Ice Moon, 105
   Ivy Moon, 182
   last quarter moon, 51
   Leo Moon, 72
   Libra Moon, 76
   Long Nights Moon, 153
   new moon, 35–36
   Old Moon, 131
   Pisces Moon, 87
   Reed Moon, 179
   Rose Moon, 113
   Rowan Moon, 161
   Sagittarius Moon, 81
   Scorpio Moon, 78
   Snow Moon, 122
   Storm Moon, 106
   Strawberry Moon, 141
   Taurus Moon, 67
   Vine Moon, 177

   Virgo Moon, 75
   waning gibbous
   moon, 48
   waxing crescent
   moon, 39
   waxing gibbous
   moon, 43
   Wolf Moon, 102
Rose Moon, 112–113
Rose Quartz
   energy clearing, 19
   first quarter moon, 41
   Hare Moon, 110, 111
   Ice Moon, 104
   Rose Moon, 112, 113
   sacred space and, 15
   Taurus Moon, 66, 67
Rowan Moon, 160–161
Ruby
   Aries Moon, 64, 65
   Blood Moon, 120
Ruby Fuchsite, 144, 145
Rutilated Quartz, 114, 115

sacred spaces, 15
   cleansing, 16, 17
   clearing, 18, 19
Sagittarius, 62, 80–81
Scolecite, 19
Scorpio, 78–79
Selenite
   energy clearing, 19
   Gemini Moon, 68, 69
   Long Nights Moon, 152
   Snow Moon, 122, 123
   Wolf Moon, 102, 103
September
   Fruit Moon, 146–147
   Harvest Moon, 118–119
   Hazel Moon, 174–175
Shattuckite, 124, 125
Shiva Lingam, 168, 169
Shungite
   Beaver Moon, 151
   Elder Moon, 181
Smoky Quartz
   Capricorn Moon, 82, 83
   Oak Moon, 170, 171

smudging, 16, 17
Snowflake Obsidian
   Old Moon, 130, 131
   waxing gibbous
   moon, 42
Snow Moon, 91, 122–123
Sodalite, 180, 181
Storm Moon, 106–107
Strawberry Moon,
140–141
Strawberry Moon-
stone, 38
Strawberry Quartz, 140
Stromatolite, 148, 149
Sunstone, 154, 155
Super Moons, 57

Tangerine Moonstone, 52
Taurus, 62, 66–67
Tugtupite, 137
Turquoise, 38

Vanadinite, 160
Variscite, 146, 147
Vine Moon, 176–177
Virgo, 74–75

waning moons
   introduction, 32
   waning crescent moon,
   46, 52–53
   waning gibbous moon,
   46, 48–49
waxing moons
   introduction, 32
   waxing crescent moon,
   38–39, 46
   waxing gibbous moon,
   42–43, 46
White Moonstone
   first quarter moon,
   40, 41
   full moon, 45
White Pearl, 183
Willow Moon, 166–167
Wolf Moon, 102–103

Yellow Sapphire, 116